PILOTS & AIRCRAFT OWNERS

LEGAL GUIDE

By

JAY C. WHITE

MEMBER, CALIFORNIA BAR

PILOTS PUBLISHERS, CO.
P. O. BOX 661
REDWOOD CITY, CALIFORNIA 94064
(415) 366-1915

TABLE OF CONTENTS

LIENS, ENCUMBRANCES AND SECURITY
INTERESTS

AVIATION CASE DIGEST SUPPLEMENT

A - AVIATION COURT CASES, GENERAL
N - NATIONAL TRANSPORTATION SAFETY BOARD
I - AVIATION INSURANCE

FOREWORD

The purpose of **PILOTS & AIRCRAFT OWNERS LEGAL GUIDE** is to acquaint pilots, aircraft owners and business operators with fundamentals of aviation law. Aviation activities have legal implications which must be considered in relation to members of the aviation community and to the community at large. This relationship is pointed out throughout the book.

TOPIC CONTENT - Topic headings will enable the reader to quickly locate subjects of interest. Since many topics are related, however, they should be reviewed together. The table of contents will often reveal several headings and sub-headings relating to a particular fact situation.

CASE CITATIONS - References to specific court cases are for illustration purposes only. They should not be used for legal guidance in individual matters.

"LEGALESE" - Since this is a publication intended mainly for persons not trained in the law an effort has been made to keep "legalese" to a minimum. Legal scholars will recognize that in certain instances more technical precision could perhaps be achieved through use of legal terms and phrases.

CAUTIONARY NOTE - For several reasons, **PILOTS & AIRCRAFT OWNERS LEGAL GUIDE** is not a "Do-it-Yourself" book. Applications of legal principles can be made only after a complete evaluation of a particular fact situation; a distinction must be drawn between facts that are of legal significance and those that are of only personal or practical significance; comprehensive review of the current law of a particular state may be essential to the solution of a legal problem; a knowledge of legal procedures is often as critical as a knowledge of the law. Procedures for the various courts and agencies vary extensively.

JAY C. WHITE

AVIATION LAW

Aviation law had its beginning long before the Wright Brothers flew their first aircraft. The first reported case was based on an unscheduled descent of a balloon which landed in a farmer's vegetable field. Curious spectators trampled the farmer's vegetables leading the farmer to sue the balloon operator for their value.

As aviation developed technically, the controlling law also developed to the point where it is today. In addition to case law, the legislatures of all states have enacted statutes that affect aviation. The federal government has likewise enacted many statutes affecting aviation. Certain federal statutes are implemented by agencies such as the Federal Aviation Administration. In terms of numbers and frequency of application the Federal Aviation Regulations are of greatest concern to persons involved as pilots, aircraft owners or aviation business operators.

GENERAL PRINCIPLES

Review of a few principles of how aviation law is made and the function our judicial system may be helpful in understanding later discussions of specific situations.

JUDGE AND JURY -- THEIR FUNCTION

In aviation court cases, as well as others, the judge decides questions of law and directs the attorneys in accordance with rules of court when presenting evidence and arguments on behalf of their clients. In certain types of cases, particularly in Federal Courts or Admiralty Courts, the judge may also decide questions of fact without the aid of a jury. In most complex cases, however, the parties have a right to have a jury decide disputed questions of fact based on evidence presented by both sides of a legal controversy.

Laymen who are called to jury duty generally have

little understanding of the various facets of aviation. Thus, it is vitally important the attorneys appearing in court have a background in aviation which will enable them to explain the fact situation in a clear and non-technical manner. Even so, a jury trial has been likened to a "crap shoot" due to the unpredictability of verdict outcome.

In a civil trial--as opposed to a criminal prosecution-- where one individual is suing another for a monetary award there are two basic questions: (1) Is the defendant legally at fault? and (2) What amount of monetary compensation is due the injured plaintiff? The jury would normally decide both after direction from the judge as to applicable law and after having heard and seen evidence presented at a trial.

In a civil trial, the plaintiff must prove his case by a "preponderance of the evidence", i.e., by convincing the jury the weight of the evidence is more than fifty percent in his favor. In their evaluation of the evidence individual jurors may give differing degrees of weight to testimony of witnesses or other items of evidence. For the plaintiff to prevail in a civil case a minimum number of jurors, e.g., 9 out of 12, must decide for the plaintiff.

In a criminal trial the prosecuting attorney has the burden of convincing the jury "beyond a reasonable doubt" of the accused person's guilt of the crime charged. For the accused to be found guilty all jurors must concur in the verdict.

NEGLIGENCE

The principle of law invoked most commonly in aviation accident cases is the law of negligence. A person is said to have been negligent when he failed to exercise a degree of care which an ordinarily prudent or reasonably careful person would have used under the same or similar circumstances. This is essentially a restatement of the commonly accepted principle that a pilot is expected to use good judgment in the operation of his aircraft.

In deciding after the fact whether a pilot has exercised the degree of care required of him by law, the courts will examine the surrounding circumstances as they existed at the time of the event, such as the pilot's level of training, weather, type of aircraft, type of operation, type of cargo, number of passengers, terrain over which he was flying, emergencies, and the type of maneuvers in which he was engaged at the time of the accident. A pilot's duty to exercise care extends to persons on the ground, his passengers, those in other aircraft and persons whose property might be damaged, and the owner of the aircraft he is flying.

If the pilot in command allows an aircraft to be operated by someone else in a negligent manner, he remains responsible even if he is not at the controls.

If the pilot legally responsible is killed in a mishap, the persons thereby injured or having their property damaged may bring suit against the deceased pilot's executor or administrator. Thus, assets of the deceased pilot's estate may be reached if there is insufficient liability insurance coverage. This is discussed further in the section on INSURANCE.

WILLFUL MISCONDUCT

A pilot may occasionally engage in conduct which is more serious than the mere failure to exercise good judgment. An example would be low level "buzzing". To justify a charge of intentional misconduct it is not necessary that the pilot have malicious or criminal intent; intentionally doing the act in disregard of safety of others will suffice. Following a particular flight, the pilot might be required to answer to criminal charges brought by the local district attorney or to a civil complaint for damage to property of a private person. He also could have his pilot certificate suspended or revoked by the FAA for violation of Federal Aviation Regulations.

During flight constituting willful misconduct, insurance relating to the aircraft would very likely not be in force since most policies apply to liability resulting from negligence only, not from intentional misconduct.

Of additional interest to the aircraft owner is the possibility the FAA may impound the aircraft. It may be held as security for any money penalty later assessed for violation of Federal Aviation Regulations. This could happen even though the owner was not piloting the aircraft. This subject is discussed further under SEIZURE OF AIRCRAFT BY FAA.

STATE LAWS -- LEGISLATIVE ACTS

Many state legislatures have modified the basic common law by enacting statutes pertaining to aviation activities. Since each state is permitted to make its own laws, so long as they are not in conflict with the Constitution or applicable Federal laws, a pilot's or aircraft owner's rights and liabilities may be considerably different depending on the particular state or states involved.

For example, a California statute imposes on the owner of an aircraft liability up to $15,000 for injury or death to a passenger, with a maximum of $30,000 for a particular accident, and $5,000 for damage to property, even though the owner is not operating the aircraft at the time of the accident.

STATE LAWS -- CASE LAW

State case law is "judge made law" resulting from individual decisions based on particular sets of facts. It is of no binding effect in a state other than that in which it is rendered. The supreme court of a given state is the final authority in state law matters not involving federal or Constitutional questions.

FEDERAL LAW

United States District Courts and Courts of Appeals have jurisdiction over many aviation cases. A decision by a given District Court or Court of Appeals is not binding in any other court of that rank unless first affirmed by a higher court.

Whenever a legal controversy arises, a determination must be made at the outset regarding the appropriate court in which to proceed. The nature of the case may permit selecting either state court or federal court. Many aviation cases are brought in federal courts due to residents of different states being plaintiffs or defendants.

CONTRIBUTORY FAULT

It is well established in many states that, except as to Workers' Compensation coverage, if a person fails to exercise reasonable care for his own safety and thereby contributes to his injury, he must bear his own loss. An example would be the injury of a passenger in the crash of an aircraft after interference by the passenger with the aircraft controls. The amount of care required of each person for his own safety is determined by the surrounding circumstances, such as his age, experience, training, weather and the time of day.

This rule may work an undue hardship on a person whose conduct has contributed only slightly to his injury. Accordingly, several states have adopted a COMPARATIVE NEGLIGENCE theory which allows an injured person to recover partial compensation if he has been only partly at fault for his injury. Although basically sound, this system sometimes presents a problem of fault apportionment for the judge or jury with resulting subjective evaluation as to the appropriate monetary compensation for the injured person.

> For example, in a Texas case a pilot
> landed his aircraft and taxied to the
> fueling area for service. After a brief

visit to the airport coffee shop, he
returned, signed a fuel receipt and
departed without personally checking
the fuel quantity. Shortly after
becoming airborne, the engine quit from
fuel starvation; the fueler had serviced
the wrong aircraft. In a suit by the
pilot against the fueler, a jury found the
pilot had contributed to his own loss by
not verifying the refueling, thus, the
fueler was not liable.

ASSUMPTION OF RISK

Another principle closely related to "Contributory
Fault" is that of "Assumption of Risk". This
means that an injured person who has voluntarily
and knowingly placed himself in a dangerous
position must bear any resulting injury or loss.
The emphasis here is on a full appreciation of the
danger involved prior to self-exposure to the
danger. An example would be the voluntary riding
as a passenger with a student pilot for the purpose
of engaging in advanced aerobatics. Another
would be the flying of an aircraft with a known
serious mechanical defect which would make it
unairworthy.

EMERGENCY ACTION

An emergency is a situation demanding immediate
action by a pilot, such as an engine failure in flight.
A pilot is not required to exercise the same
standard of performance in an emergency situation
as is required under normal circumstances. An
error in judgment on his part during an emergency is
not necessarily a basis for incurring legal liability
if an accident occurs. The pilot will not be relieved
of liability, however, if his previous careless
conduct created the emergency situation. For
example, if an engine fails due to inadequate
preflight inspection, the pilot will be held
responsible for any resulting damage or injury
incurred during an emergency landing.

In a Texas case the Court found that the crash of a Cessna 210 near the Greater Southwest Airport was due to the pilot's fault only. The aircraft occupied by the pilot only had been flown on a ferry flight from Atlanta to the Dallas area where weather conditions were poor. Following one missed approach, the pilot requested an Airport Surveillance Radar approach, advising the Controller of a 20-minute fuel supply remaining. Although he was thereafter given priority handling, the pilot was unable to complete the approach following fuel exhaustion and crashed in a wooded area short of the airport. The Court held that, although the pilot had experienced an emergency situation due to low fuel supply, it was of his own making, since he had failed earlier to divert to a suitable airport while his fuel supply was adequate. Thus, the Controller and the U. S. government were not at fault.

This discussion of civil liability in emergency situations is not to be confused with the pilot's "Emergency Authority" respecting non-compliance with Federal Aviation Regulations. In the latter the pilot must be prepared to prove his action was warranted by the urgency of the situation if he is to be excused for violating a regulation, and that his own bad judgment did not bring about the emergency.

ACT OF GOD

Aircraft accidents occasionally happen even though all the persons involved exercise reasonable care in every respect. If human care and foresight cannot guard against an unforeseen accident, the pilot is, in theory, not usually responsible for injury or damage caused thereby. In application, however, this theory is not always easy to apply; if a natural elemental force, such as turbulence, is a factor in an accident, the pilot may have been negligent in failing to anticipate the foreseeable consequence of flight in the area. Moreover, what may appear to be an Act of God may have arisen due to prior negligence of the pilot, in which case the pilot would still be responsible. This type of situation often arises where adverse weather is a substantial factor and the pilot's judgmental call is later brought into question.

Also, certain states, such as California, have to a certain extent abrogated ACT OF GOD as a defense to liability by an aircraft owner for injury or damage caused by his aircraft. This is discussed further under STATE LAWS -- LEGISLATIVE ACTS and OWNERSHIP OF AIRCRAFT.

EMPLOYER'S LIABILITY FOR PILOT'S ACTS

On the theory that a pilot is an agent of his employer, acts occurring during the pursuit of the pilot's employment are frequently imputed to his employer. The employer is liable for injury to persons or damage to property resulting from the pilot's failure to exercise reasonable care in carrying out his duties of employment.

In application, however, this is not as simple as it may sound. Questions often arise as to whether the pilot was acting in the course of his employment at the time of the negligent acts leading to the accident or incident.

> For example, a corporation-owned aircraft being piloted by the corporation president stalled and crashed shortly after takeoff. All of the passengers on board were injured. When suit was brought against the corporation, the evidence produced at the trial indicated the president was not engaged in corporate business at the time of the accident, but had been on a personal mission for the purpose of

sightseeing with his guests. Thus, the
pilot was liable, but his employer was
not.

A pilot may be considered an employee, making his
employer liable for negligent acts even though the
pilot is flying his own aircraft. The essential
question for any given flight is whether or not the
pilot is an independent contractor responsible only
for doing a job or accomplishing a task but not
subject to direction and control from the person for
whom he is doing the work as to how it is to be
achieved. If he is subject to supervision and
control, he is generally classified as an employee.

A person may be liable for acts of an independent
contractor if the one for whom the work is being
done fails to use adequate care in selecting a
competent contractor for the task involved.

For example, in an Arizona case, a
beekeeper lost a major part of his apiary
from drifting poison after an aircraft
sprayed an adjacent lettuce field. The
owner of the lettuce field was required
to pay for the bees although he
contended he should not be liable since
the pilot who did the spraying was an
independent contractor rather than an
employee of the field owner.

This case points out an additional important rule
relating to relationships between persons,
namely, a person cannot escape legal responsibility
for results results of a dangerous operation by
merely delegating the work to someone else.

As a practical matter, since the employer is more
likely than the pilot to have assets and insurance
coverage sufficient to satisfy a judgment, an
injured person, or one having his property damaged,
will usually attempt to show that the pilot was an
employee rather than an independent contractor.
It must be borne in mind, however, if the employer
is legally liable, the negligent pilot will be liable

also if he personally committed the wrongful act.

See the sections on WORKERS' COMPENSATION INSURANCE and AIRCRAFT OWNERSHIP for additional information relative to this subject.

PROPERTY DAMAGE

Property damage occurring during aircraft accidents may be of one or more forms, such as damage to the aircraft being flown, other aircraft, buildings, utility lines, livestock and other animals, timber and crops. Under certain state laws, the owner of an aircraft is liable for any damage caused by it even if the pilot was not negligent. For example, the owner of buildings damaged in a crash following engine failure would be entitled to compensation from the aircraft owner.

Aircraft often collide with wires and poles in the vicinity of airports. Although the owner of the poles and wires, under certain circumstances, could be liable for personal injury and aircraft damage resulting from the collision, the situation could be reversed imposing on the pilot or aircraft owner liability for damage to the poles and wires. Whenever such a collision occurs, a thorough evaluation of the facts is necessary to determine who is at fault. The owner can be held liable for allowing poles and wires to remain where they could reasonably be expected to endanger aircraft if no adequate warnings are given of their presence. It is not necessary, however, that poles or wires be marked so long as they are clearly visible to the pilot. In any event, the pilot must exercise due care for property of others by maintaining adequate altitude for the particular portion of the approach or departure pattern.

MONETARY COMPENSATION FOR INJURY, DEATH, OR PROPERTY DAMAGE

Several factors are involved in determination of the amount of monetary compensation for injury, death or property damage. Direct out-of-pocket expenses, such as medical expenses, hospitalization, and loss of wages or salary during a period of recuperation are compensable. If there is permanent disability, compensation is based on the degree to which the disability will likely affect the injured person's normal activities. Recovery by heirs of a deceased person is based on loss of future support and other economic benefits as well as loss of the intangibles of love, affection and companionship.

Recovery by an injured person is also allowed in many cases for the element of pain and suffering. Due to its subjective nature this often presents difficulty for a jury in the computation of an exact monetary figure.

For damage to property, recovery is allowed for depreciation based on value immediately before the accident as compared with value immediately after the accident. If the property is a total loss, recovery is for full market value. If the property damaged is being used in a business undertaking for the production of income, such as an aircraft that is being used for charter purposes, recovery is allowed for loss of use of that property during a reasonable period in which repairs are being made; if the aircraft is completely destroyed, in some states recovery is allowed for loss of use for a reasonable period during which a replacement is being acquired.

In addition, some states allow recovery for loss of use of a personal aircraft not used for business purposes.

Following an aircraft accident, recovery of compensation may be allowed for one or more of the following:

1. Death of a passenger

2. Death of a crew member

3. Pain and suffering of any injured person

4.   Loss of earnings, past and future

5.   Medical, hospital, physicians' and related
     expenses

6.   Loss of aircraft

7.   Damage to aircraft

8.   Loss of use of aircraft for business or
     nonbusiness purposes

9.   Damage to property on the ground

10. Death or injury of person on the ground

11. Loss of future support by family members of
     deceased or severely injured person, either
     passenger or crew member

PAYMENT OF JUDGMENT

Whenever injury, death or property damage results
from an accident, a question immediately arises as
to who is to pay the judgment if the plaintiff is
successful in proving his right to compensation. In
a majority of cases an insurance carrier will
ultimately pay the judgment. If, however, the
defendant has no liability insurance, or has
inadequate coverage, his assets are subject to levy
and sale. The same applies to the assets of the
estate of a pilot who meets his demise in an
accident in which he is legally at fault.

It is vitally important for an employee-pilot's
protection that his employer have adequate
insurance to cover the pilot's liability.
Regrettably, many small commercial flying
operators do not have adequate coverage. This
may be due to business economic necessity of
keeping operating costs down, or to the failure to
understand insurance needs for the particular flight
operation.

It is clearly in the individual pilot's economic

interest, whether flying commercially or privately, to assure himself of liability insurance coverage to protect his assets, future earnings and other acquisitions. A personal liability policy can be purchased for this purpose.

CONTRACT LAW (AGREEMENTS)

A contract is an agreement that is legally enforceable in a court of law. Contractual agreements arise often when persons such as pilots, aircraft owners and business operators purchase insurance, purchase an aircraft, rent tie-down space, rent or lease aircraft, join flying clubs, etc.

Although not all contracts are required to be in writing to be enforceable, disagreements are less likely to arise if there is a written memorandum showing intent of the parties as to details of the agreement. If no written agreement is available, proof of a contract and its details would have to be established by oral testimony and other documentation. Should legal action be required, a written document is very desirable as evidence of the agreement. As a practical matter, a written document is desirable as a memorandum to aid the relatively frail memory of even the most honest of persons. This is discussed further under the section on AIRCRAFT SALE, PURCHASE, FINANCING.

An often troublesome type of contract is an unwritten or poorly written partnership agreement. A partnership is dissolved by law upon death of a partner, and can be dissolved if one partner withdraws from the agreement voluntarily. Disputes tend to arise upon dissolution of the partnership if there is no written agreement stating clearly what disposition is to be made of assets, liability for debts, etc.

Joint ownership of aircraft is based on an agreement, written, oral or implied, between the various co-owners. If ownership is through a corporation, for example, an incorporated flying club, the articles of incorporation, bylaws and operations rules constitute the agreement. See FLYING CLUBS.

An aircraft insurance policy is a special form of written contract which often leads to difficulties in respect to interpretation and coverage. This is discussed further under the section on INSURANCE.

AIRCRAFT OPERATION

The various phases of routine flight, namely, flight planning, preflight inspection, taxi, takeoff, enroute, approach and landing, have one thing in common: they require the pilot to use good judgment. If an accident occurs, the pilot's judgment is evaluated in retrospect. This evaluation is often referred to as "Monday morning quarterbacking".

FLIGHT PLANNING

The basis of any successful flight is a well thought-out flight plan; regrettably this frequently is the most neglected phase. In retrospective evaluation, many accidents have their genesis in inadequate preflight planning. Common deficiencies include failure to:

1. Review enroute and destination weather

2. Review alternate airport weather

3. Plan for possible need of an alternate airport

4. Obtain adequate checkout in the particular type aircraft

5. Review minimum enroute altitudes with respect to single engine performance of twin engine aircraft

6. Review available airports for enroute emergency use

14

7. Review weight and balance of aircraft

8. Review decreased aircraft and engine
performance during high temperatures

9. Review decreased aircraft and engine
performance at high elevation airports

10. Allow sufficient time for unanticipated
delay, thus, resulting in continued
flight with unwarranted risks

11. Arrange an adequate rest period prior
to flight

12. Abstain from alcoholic beverages for a
reasonable period prior to flight

13. Review information regarding navigational
facilities, runway lights, airport
construction, etc., and,

14. Appraise objectively the individual
pilot's experience, skill and ability
to complete the particular flight.

For example, in a Wisconsin case
involving the crash of a Piper at night,
the jury decided the pilot had not
exercised reasonable care for the safety
of his passengers since (1) he had
previous reports that weather enroute
was adverse, but, nevertheless,
attempted the flight; (2) he failed to
set his altimeter properly and was flying
170 feet lower than it indicated and, (3)
due to lack of adequate rest prior to the
flight, he apparently fell asleep while
piloting the plane.

PREFLIGHT INSPECTION

A reasonably complete preflight inspection to
assure airworthiness is part of the procedure in
successfully operating any type of aircraft. For

the pilot's personal and legal protection, this inspection must be such as the surrounding circumstances dictate. It will vary from one type or one individual aircraft to another.

In a Nebraska case a pilot started a flight after completing a cursory inspection of his fabric covered aircraft which had been parked for several days during periods of heavy rainfall. Shortly after becoming airborne, he lost control and crashed due to an extremely tail-heavy condition of the aircraft. His passenger was severely injured. The investigation revealed that water entering through the canopy had collected in the tail section due to clogging of the drain grommets. The jury decided the pilot had been negligent in not having inspected the grommets by use of an object such as a pencil.

In an Oregon case a pilot and his passengers were injured in the crash of their aircraft when the engine failed shortly after takeoff due to lack of sufficient fuel in the tanks. Investigation revealed a preflight inspection had been made by the pilot before dawn without the aid of a light. The jury concluded that the pilot was negligent since he should have inspected his fuel quantity by use of a "stick or a flashlight".

On the other hand, in an Alabama case a pilot who had rented an aircraft and made a preflight inspection crashed shortly after takeoff due to the controls becoming jammed. Investigation revealed the malfunction was caused by a small screwdriver which had been left beneath the floorboards by the aircraft owner's mechanic. Since this hazard

was not of a nature that it would be
revealed by a reasonable preflight
inspection, the pilot was not at fault,
but, rather the aircraft owner was
liable for injuries to the pilot.

TAXI

If an accident occurs on the ground, a question may
arise as to whether the aircraft was taxiing or
whether it was moving for the purpose of take-off,
or from the impetus of a landing. This
determination may be critical in respect to
insurance coverage. Aircraft insurance policies
often cover one phase but not the other, and
deductibles are different for different phases.
Also, different Federal Aviation Regulations may
apply.

During taxi movement the pilot is expected to
maintain a reasonable lookout to prevent injury to
others or damage to their property. Surrounding
circumstances, such as type of aircraft, any blind
spots in the structural configuration, and amount of
lighting will determine the amount of caution and
type of maneuvers required. For example, a slower
speed would be expected if the aircraft being moved
were a "tail dragger" rather than one with tricycle
landing gear affording better visibility and
maneuverability.

In an early precedent-setting California
case a student pilot collided with a
parked DC-3 while taxiing a Luscombe.
The court required him to pay the repair
cost of $2950 plus $7500 for loss of
profit which the owner would have made
if the DC-3 had not been damaged.

TAKEOFF

Since the takeoff portion is a very critical phase of
flight, the pilot is expected to employ good
judgment as well as reasonable flying skill. His
performance will be judged in light of such

surrounding circumstances as the prevailing wind
and weather, along with preflight preparation
precautions.

For example, in a Louisiana case a pilot
continued a takeoff in a twin engine
Beechcraft even though one engine was
backfiring and failed after lift off.
For the ensuing crash in a field, killing
a cotton picker, the pilot was held
liable for the death.

In a Missouri case the pilot of a Cessna
carrying three passengers attempted a
short field takeoff utilizing a flap
setting of 40 degrees instead of the
recommended 20 degrees. The pilot
was held liable for the ensuing crash.

In a Wisconsin case judgment was
rendered against a pilot's estate after
he and his passenger had been killed
shortly after takeoff. The aircraft had
struck a row of trees after the pilot had
attempted to take off with the wing
flaps in the full down position.

ENROUTE

Although a majority of accidents occur in the
vicinity of the departure airport or the arrival
airport, enroute accidents occasionally happen.
These accidents may result from poor pilot
judgment in flight planning combined with faulty
flying technique.

For example, in a Washington case an
aircraft, while flying at 100 feet above
the water, struck transmission wires
strung between the mainland and an
island. The wires had been placed there
by the United States Coast Guard and
were unmarked. In a suit against the
Government, the pilot lost. The jury
decided the pilot did not exercise

reasonable care for his own safety nor
the safety of property of others since he
did not familiarize himself with the area
before attempting such low-level
flying.

In an early Nevada case involving a
collision between an airline aircraft and
an Air Force fighter, the judge stated a
very significant and still current
principle: "Even though an aircraft is
being operated on an IFR flight plan,
the pilot is under a legal obligation
when flying in VFR conditions to see
and avoid other aircraft." In this case
both the U. S. Government and the
airline were legally liable for deaths of
the airline passengers since both
aircraft were being flown in VFR
conditions at the time of collision.

APPROACH AND LANDING

The term "landing" usually refers to the operation
of the aircraft from the time it commences to lose
altitude in the vicinity of the airport with the
purpose of touching down on land or water, until it
has stopped moving along the surface from the
impetus of the descent. Although this definition
may appear academic, it is of controlling
significance for insurance purposes if a policy
covers "flight" damage or "taxi" damage but not
both.

The approach and landing phase presents
opportunities for error. It demands good inflight
planning as well as flying skill. Frequent errors
include:

1. Selecting an inadequate runway

2. Failure to keep a proper lookout for
    other aircraft

3. Failure to adequately review airport
    approach information

4. Failure to follow proper traffic patterns

5. Failure to yield the right-of-way in accordance with Federal Aviation Regulations

6. Using an approach profile too steep or too shallow

7. Striking objects such as poles or wires in the approach path

8. Attempting to land when the visibility is inadequate

9. Landing at excessive or inadequate airspeed

10. Landing with excessive crosswind or tailwind

11. Failure to use checklist

12. Failure to observe aircraft operating requirements

For example, in an early Tennessee case involving the crash of a DC-3, the pilot apparently attempted to make an IFR approach even though previous aircraft logbook reports indicated the aircraft's navigational radios were unreliable. In a suit brought against the pilot's employer, the jury decided the pilot had not exercised reasonable care for the safety of his passengers. The airline was liable on the principle that the pilot was an agent of his employer and acting within the scope of his employment at the time of the accident.

In a California case a non-instrument rated pilot was found liable for the resulting crash when he attempted to make a VFR descent through a selected hole in a broken cloud layer with ensuing loss of control.

In an Illinois case relating to an accident at an airport having no control tower, a landing aircraft collided with a taxiing aircraft. Although Federal Aviation Regulations gave the landing aircraft the right-of-way over aircraft moving on the ground, the pilot of the landing aircraft was found to be at fault. Since the taxiing aircraft was painted a bright canary yellow and was plainly visible, the court found the landing pilot had failed to maintain an adequate lookout, otherwise, he would have observed the taxiing plane and would have been able to avoid the collision.

In a Georgia case the pilot of a Beech Bonanza attempted a pull-up after approaching at too high an altitude to permit a landing. The aircraft mushed, stalled, crashed and burned. Evidence introduced at the trial indicated the pilot had used faulty technique in that he had attempted to execute a pull-up with the propeller control in the high pitch position.

In a Minnesota case a collision between a Cessna 195 and a Cessna 210 occurred while they were on final approach at an uncontrolled airport. The 195 came from behind and above, contacting and shearing off the tail of the 210. Although both pilots were killed, the owner of the 210 sued the owner of the 195 and secured a favorable judgment for loss of the 210. The reason given by the court was violation of Federal Aviation Regulations by the pilot of the 195 pertaining to "right-of-way while converging, overtaking and landing".

CROP DUSTING AND SPRAYING

Due to the special hazards involved, dusting or

spraying must be conducted with due regard for the rights of adjoining property owners. Potential damage by a low flying aircraft, as well as from chemicals being used, requires the operator to use special care in respect to his neighbor. He must use due care to see that the airplane spreading the materials holds off the spray when making turns over the crops or property of others; that dusting operations are not conducted when any breeze could float the spray onto the property of others; and that the aircraft does not cause personal injury or property damage.

> For example, in an unusual North Dakota case a duster pilot had landed on a public highway as a matter of convenience to refuel and pick up additional spray. Suit was brought against him by a passenger injured in an automobile which ran off the highway to avoid colliding with the duster airplane. The pilot was found liable under the applicable North Dakota law which stated: "Any person who wrongfully renders a public highway dangerous for travel by placing obstructions thereon must respond in damages to anyone injured in consequence of such obstruction."

BUZZING/LOW ALTITUDE FLYING

Aside from disregard of his own safety when flying at very low altitudes, a pilot should consider one or more of the following possible adverse results:

1. Violation of state law imposing criminal sanctions.

2. Violation of Federal Aviation Regulations leading to license suspension or revocation.

3. Civil suit against him for damage to property or injury to persons.

4. Lack of insurance coverage during such
    flight.

Federal Aviation Regulations specifying certain
minimum flight altitudes have been issued with the
object of avoiding injury to persons on the ground
or damage to their property; to protect the pilot
from collision with stationary objects; and to give
him an opportunity to pick an emergency landing
area in the event of engine or other mechanical
malfunction.

> In an early Pennsylvania case the pilot
> of a Piper collided with a transmission
> line over the Susquehanna River while
> flying at an altitude of 125 feet. In a
> suit by the pilot's widow against the
> power and light corporation which
> owned the transmission line, she was not
> allowed to collect for the death of the
> pilot. Although the lines were not
> marked, their position was such that
> they would not interfere with aircraft
> in ordinary flight. Thus, through
> failure to use due care for his own
> safety, legally the pilot was solely
> responsible for his demise.
>
> In a Minnesota case a farmer was
> seriously injured when his hay mower
> was pulled over him by his horses after
> they had been frightened by a low flying
> FAA Beechcraft. The aircraft was
> being flown just above the tree tops in
> aerial survey work. The court found
> that even though the pilots had been
> required to do low level flying, they had
> not been relieved of their duty to
> exercise reasonable care and precaution
> so as not to injure persons on the
> ground. Thus, since the pilots were
> agents of the United States
> Government, the Government was
> responsible for the farmer's injuries.

> In a similar Louisiana case, a farmer
> was seriously injured by the sickle of his
> hay mower when his horses were
> frightened by a low flying government
> helicopter. The Government was
> required to compensate the farmer for
> his injuries.

These two cases last cited should not, however, be construed to mean the U. S. Government is always liable for acts of its pilots. To a certain extent the Government is immune from liability under the ancient theory, "The King can do no wrong." This is discussed further under GOVERNMENT LIABILITY.

MID-AIR COLLISION

Many aviation legal problems are related to the "see and avoid" concept. A principle which many pilots consider to be unrealistic is that which places the primary responsibility on the shoulders of a pilot flying in VFR conditions to see and avoid other aircraft even though he may be flying a high-speed aircraft on an IFR flight plan. A pilot is not relieved of his responsibility to "see and avoid" when flying in VFR conditions even though an airways traffic controller may have a duty to provide adequate traffic separation or to provide traffic information.

If a mid-air collision is preceded by violation of a Federal Aviation Regulation, there will likely be a strong inference that the pilot in violation failed to exercise a reasonable degree of care. Following such an accident, it is not uncommon for suit to be brought against the pilot, his employer, and the United States Government since all three may be legally partly at fault.

Persons who may be entitled to compensation following a collision include the pilot not at fault, or his heirs, persons aboard either aircraft or their heirs, owner of either aircraft, persons on the ground who are injured or have their property damaged.

SONIC BOOM

A sonic boom can generally be described as a combined pressure and sound wave generated by an object moving through the air at speeds equal to or exceeding that of sound. Adverse effects to persons on the ground may include:

1. Personal injury

2. Damage to their property

3. Substantial and unreasonable interference with use and enjoyment of their property

Although liability for such damage or injury is based on negligence or willful misconduct of the owner or operator of an aircraft, certain practical problems make recovery of compensation difficult. The person bringing suit must be able to identify the responsible plane, to trace the damaging operation to a particular flight, and prove the nature and amount of his injury or damage.

If the aircraft involved is a military aircraft, there may be an additional factor which would preclude recovery of compensation: The Government is to a certain extent immune from suit. Generally, this means no monetary recovery can be had if the military pilot conducts his flight in a reasonable manner in keeping with a proper discretionary order of his superior. The distinction between discretionary and ministerial government functions is not entirely clear and often must be determined, on a case by case basis, in light of the particular circumstances involved. The Government is not immune to suit for negligently performed ministerial acts of its employees.

Sonic boom damage has also presented problems respecting insurance coverage for property damage.

> For example, in a Texas case a farm
> building was caused to collapse by a

sonic boom created by a low flying Navy aircraft. The farmer submitted an insurance claim based on a provision of his insurance policy relating to "damage caused by aircraft". The insurance company refused to pay, contending this damage was not the type of damage covered by the policy. In a suit against his insurance company the farmer won.

AIR SHOWS

Activities associated with air shows often lend themselves to legal implications, largely due to the many different group and individual functions.

The law places on the proprietor of an airport or an airfield the obligation to see that it is safe for such aircraft as are entitled to use it; to give an appropriate warning to pilots of any danger of which the proprietor knows or should know. The proprietor also has a legal duty to keep the premises in a reasonably safe condition for those persons who come there by expressed or implied invitation.

A person or an organization giving flying exhibitions or hosting a fly-in has a duty to exercise due care to make the place and the exhibitions safe for spectators and patrons.

In an early North Carolina case an agricultural association was held liable for physical, nervous system and mental suffering of a 53 year old man who was carried aloft and transported about 1-1/2 miles. His foot had become entangled in a rope attached to a balloon during an unscheduled and unexpected ascent. The sponsoring association had previously advertised a "free balloon ascension" as one of the attractions for that day, but apparently failed to warn interested members of the public against associated dangers.

In a later North Carolina case a pilot's estate was found liable after the pilot failed to recover from a spin demonstration, killing himself as well as his passenger. The previously agreed upon maneuver was for a precision spin to start at 2,000 feet, and for three to five turns to be made. Instead, he commenced the spin at 1,800 feet, making 4-1/2 turns before contacting the ground.

OWNERSHIP OF AIRCRAFT

The owner or operator of an aircraft is bound to use reasonable care to prevent injury to persons or damage to their property. Since "reasonable care" must be commensurate with the dangerous consequences to be reasonably expected, the amount of care required can vary; it may be a very high degree of care under some circumstances and only a slight degree of care under others.

In addition, certain individual states, such as California, have enacted statutes imposing civil liability on the owner of an aircraft which causes injury or property damage irrespective of the owner's fault.

Otherwise, the basic legal principles to be applied are the common-law Rules of Negligence -- the burden being on the person who has suffered injury or damage to prove the fault of the owner or operator as the legal cause of the accident.

Under the Civil Penalty Provision of the Federal Aviation Act of 1958, a non-operator owner can be held liable for FAR violations although not personally flying the aircraft. The owner who authorizes a pilot to use his plane becomes liable for violations of certain FARs by the pilot. But if

the legal owner has leased the airplane under a bona
fide lease for a period of thirty days or more, he is
not liable under this provision of the Act unless he
has actual possession or control of the plane at the
time of the violation.

AIRCRAFT PURCHASE, SALE, TITLE RECORDING

The Federal Aviation Act established a system of
registration and recordation designed to protect
the various interests in aircraft, such as title,
financing mortgages and liens for labor and
materials furnished in repair. The purpose of
recording provisions of the Act is to give notice and
to protect the interests of persons who have dealt
on faith of the recorded title of an aircraft and as
to whom it would be an injustice to give effect to
unrecorded interests of other persons. The person
who in good faith and without knowledge of an
unrecorded interest is first to record his interest
with the FAA Aircraft Registry Office in Oklahoma
City will have priority over subsequently recorded
conflicting interests.

PROSPECTIVE BUYER'S PRELIMINARY INVESTI-GATION

Before committing himself to purchase, the
prospective purchaser should secure a Title Search
of the aircraft records from the Aircraft Registry
Office of the FAA in Oklahoma City. This search
can be secured through one of several private
organizations who are in the business of providing
that service, and who can be identified through
advertisements in various aviation publications.
The FAA should not be contacted directly for this
information since the workload of the Registry
Office precludes the required research.

As a result of the Title Search, the prospective
purchaser will receive information relating to:

1. The present registered owner, thus
    determining who is to sign the Bill of
    Sale;

2. Identity of mortgage or lien holders who
   must be paid at the time of the sale and
   who must execute a release to be filed by
   the new owner with the FAA;

3. Identity of the previous owner or owners
   with whom the purchaser may desire to
   consult respecting history of the aircraft
   relating to such things as accidents and
   maintenance.

The title search procedure is of utmost importance
if the buyer wants an "unclouded" title to his
aircraft. "Clouds", such as any mortgage, prior
sale, lien or other document on record could result
in the purchaser losing the aircraft as well as his
purchase money.

Additional documents which should be inspected
prior to any commitment to purchase are the Bill
of Sale, Airworthiness Certificate, Engine and
Aircraft Log Books, other maintenance records,
maintenance manual, service letters or bulletins,
aircraft flight manual and written evidence in log
books that all FAA airworthiness directives and
manufacturer's bulletins have been complied with.

WRITTEN AGREEMENT RELATING TO PURCHASE

A final preparatory step should be the drafting of a
brief written contract for the purchase of the
aircraft. This document should be reviewed in
detail by both purchaser and seller prior to
signature. If the transaction is to be an "as is"
sale with the seller making no warranties or
assurances regarding the aircraft, this should be
clearly stated.

The document should contain legal name and mailing
addresses of seller and buyer; identification of the
aircraft by registration and serial numbers; a
statement of price, terms, financing; any special or
contingency conditions; a statement as to when
title and possession are to be transferred to the
buyer.

If there is to be a warranty representation by the seller that the aircraft is in an airworthy condition meeting all requirements of Federal Aviation Regulations this should be stated.

There can be a complete listing of any defects or deficiencies in the aircraft for which the seller is to be either responsible or relieved of responsibility; there can be a statement by the seller that, except for the noted defects or deficiencies, the airplane, its engine, accessories and appliances have been carefully and thoroughly examined and tested in accordance with the testing and examination procedures used by first-class aircraft repair stations; an included statement can require the seller to take all steps necessary to register the aircraft in records of the FAA and deliver the aircraft to the buyer with title free and clear of liens or other encumbrances.

A statement can be included requiring that any controversy or claim arising out of the transaction will be settled by arbitration in accordance with rules of the American Arbitration Association and associated legal proceedings required to implement an award of that association.

An enforcement provision can be included which would require payment of attorney fees by the party at fault in the event either party is required to take legal action to enforce the agreement.

This agreement should be dated and signed by buyer, seller and at least one disinterested witness.

TRANSFER OF AIRCRAFT TITLE

The procedure for taking title to a newly acquired aircraft requires the buyer to submit to the FAA Aircraft Registry facility in Oklahoma City two documents:

1. A bill of sale signed by the seller,

2. An application for aircraft registration signed by the new owner.

In addition, a third document is required if a claim based on a mortgage or lien has been satisfied; namely, a release signed by a third party who held the security interest. Until the FAA receives this signed release, the records will not be cleared of the encumbrance.

It is to be noted a speedy recording of the completed documents is desirable since the date of filing is the date which determines the priority of any documents or instruments representing conflicts of interest.

OTHER RECORDABLE INTEREST

In addition to "title", other recordable interests include chattel mortgages, conditional sales contracts, security agreements, liens for labor and materials used in improving or repairing an aircraft and any other interest affecting the title of an aircraft.

TITLE SEARCH BY LENDER

A lending institution contemplating the financing of an aircraft purchase should secure a title search prior to making any loan commitment. The lender will want to know that when it makes the loan and takes a mortgage, it will have a first lien against the aircraft.

RENTING OR LOANING AIRCRAFT TO ANOTHER

Renting or loaning aircraft may impose liability on the owner for injury or damage to two classes of persons: (1) the person who has possession, and (2) other persons who may be injured by the aircraft.

Although the fact of mere ownership did not impose liability on the owner of an aircraft according to the basic common-law, there are several exceptions which may make the owner liable:

1. A mechanical defect in the aircraft or its

component parts may have been the legal cause of injury.

2. The owner may have been negligent in permitting an unqualified pilot to operate the aircraft.

3. The pilot may have been an agent or employee of the owner.

4. Individual state law may impose liability on the owner irrespective of the operative fact situation.

5. The Federal Aviation Administrator may assess a money penalty against the owner for violation of FARs.

> In an early New Hampshire case the owner of an aircraft was found liable under a state statute imposing liability on any person who "causes or authorizes" operation of an aircraft. The renter pilot had operated the aircraft improperly, frightening a horse which in turn struck and injured a child.

It must be borne in mind, however, an injured pilot may have been contributorily at fault in wrongful operation of the aircraft or he may have assumed the risk of a known defect. Thus, he would be legally responsible for his own injuries. This contributory fault by the pilot or his knowledge of such defect would not, however, relieve the owner of liability to third persons such as passengers.

AIRCRAFT MAINTENANCE BY OWNER OR PILOT

Federal Aviation Regulations Part 43 authorizes the holder of a pilot certificate to perform PREVENTIVE MAINTENANCE on any aircraft owned or operated by him that is not used for commercial service.

Although this function can effect a very substantial savings in both expense and time, it should be done with prudence. An initial determination is required to classify the proposed maintenance as "preventive" rather than "major". Work of the following type is stated by Part 43 to be preventive maintenance:

1. Removal, installation, and repair of landing gear tires.

2. Replacing elastic shock absorber cords on landing gear.

3. Servicing landing gear shock struts by adding oil, air or both.

4. Servicing landing gear wheel bearings, such as cleaning and greasing.

5. Replacing defective safety wiring or cotter keys.

6. Lubrication not requiring disassembly other than removal of nonstructural items such as cover plates, cowlings and fairings.

7. Making simple fabric patches not requiring rib stitching or the removal of structural parts or control surfaces.

8. Replenishing hydraulic fluid in the hydraulic reservoir.

9. Refinishing the decorative coating of fuselage, wings, tail group surfaces (excluding balanced control surfaces), fairings, cowling, landing gear, cabin or cockpit interior when removal or disassembly of any primary structure or operating system is not required.

10. Applying preservative or protective material to components where the disassembly of any primary structure or operating system is not involved and where such coating is not prohibited or is not contrary to good practices.

11. Repairing upholstery and decorative furnishings of the cabin or cockpit interior when the repairing does not require disassembly of any primary structure or operating system or affect primary structure of the aircraft.

12. Making small simple repairs to fairings, nonstructural cover plates, cowlings, and small patches and reinforcements not changing the contour so as to interfere with proper airflow.

13. Replacing side windows where that work does not interfere with the structure of any operating system such as controls, electrical equipment, etc.

14. Replacing safety belts.

15. Replacing seats or seat parts with replacement parts approved for the aircraft, not involving disassembly or any primary structure or operating system.

16. Trouble shooting and repairing broken circuits in landing light wiring circuits.

17. Replacing bulbs, reflectors and lenses of position and landing lights.

18. Replacing wheels and skis where no weight and balance computation is involved.

19. Replacing any cowling not requiring removal of the propeller or disconnection of flight controls.

20. Replacing or cleaning spark plugs and setting of spark plug gap clearance.

21. Replacing any hose connection except hydraulic connection.

22. Replacing prefabricated fuel lines.

23. Cleaning fuel and oil strainers.

24. Replacing batteries and checking fluid level and specific gravity.

25. Removing and installing glider wings and tail surfaces that are specifically designed for quick removal and installation and when such removal and installation can be accomplished by the pilot.

Confirmation as to classification as "preventive" of a particular item of maintenance can be made by contacting a maintenance inspector of the local FAA General Aviation District Office or by consulting a licensed A&P mechanic or aircraft inspector.

Aside from the obvious matter of safety, there are at least two other reasons for limiting action to preventive maintenance and not transgressing to "major" maintenance or "alterations": (1) there may be a violation of FARs, and (2) insurance coverage for the aircraft may be affected.

FIXED BASE OPERATOR (AIRPORT SERVICES OPERATOR)

Due to varying activities in which a fixed base operator may be involved, discussions contained elsewhere herein under such headings as FLYING SCHOOL OPERATIONS, RENTING AIRCRAFT, REPAIR, MAINTENANCE and AIRPORT OWNER-SHIP may be applicable.

> In a Pennsylvania case the owner of a Piper paid a monthly fee for the privilege of using the fixed based operator's tie-down facilities. He discovered on a Monday morning that the entire front portion of his aircraft had disappeared over the weekend. Everything forward of the cabin--the engine and its fittings, cowling, propeller and nosewheel assembly--had apparently been removed by an energetic thief. In a suit brought by

the aircraft owner against the fixed base operator the FBO was found not at fault. He had merely rented space to the aircraft owner and did not have possession of the aircraft; further, under the circumstances he had used reasonable care and was not required to guard the aircraft from theft.

In a Texas case an aircraft was destroyed by fire while it was being repaired. The owner brought suit against the repairman, alleging he had been negligent in not protecting the aircraft. In a rather surprising decision the jury found that the repairman had exercised a proper degree of care even though he, (1) heated the fabric covered aircraft with an electric lamp, (2) left the aircraft unattended while it was being doped and heated, and (3) failed to turn off the master electric switch while he was away from the aircraft.

Contrast these two cases with others cited under AIRPORT OWNERSHIP OR OPERATION where operators were found liable for damage to aircraft.

MANUFACTURE, REPAIR and MAINTENANCE of AIRCRAFT

While an aircraft is no longer considered an inherently dangerous vehicle, it becomes a thing of danger unless it is manufactured, repaired and maintained without serious mechanical faults or defects. If such faults or defects exist, the zone of danger includes all persons who may use the aircraft or be in the vicinity of its use.

A repair shop may be required to inspect an aircraft as part of its operations. Here, too, negligence in the manner of performing any inspections and failure to detect and correct, or to warn the owner of dangerous conditions, may subject the repair facility to liability for subsequent injuries or damage. A legal duty exists to perform satisfactory inspections utilizing industry-wide accepted practices and procedures.

A repair facility has a duty to exercise reasonable care to protect an airplane left in its possession for repairs, and to return the plane to the owner in at least as good condition as when it was received. Liability for any damage or loss while the plane is in the repairer's possession turns upon the question of the presence or absence of the repairer's negligence.

> In an early Ohio case setting a precedent which is still followed today, a Ford Tri-Motor owned by American Airways took off from the Cincinnati Airport. Two pilots and four passengers were aboard. While still in initial stages of climb out an object was seen to fall from the aircraft. It was a propeller blade. This loss caused a vibration of the right engine which then tore free of its mounts in a matter of seconds. Simultaneously the remaining blade cut through the aileron control cables, allowing the aircraft to stall and fall to earth.
>
> Investigation disclosed that the propeller hub was broken. An overhaul facility had reconditioned the propeller three months prior to the crash, but had overlooked the presence of tool marks on the inner surface of the hub. These marks increased the probability of a fatigue failure.
>
> In a suit brought by the airline against the repair facility the judge ruled that, since the tool marks could have been discovered during a reasonable inspection, and since the overhauler

knew from maintenance work on other propellers of the same model that the marks were a source of grave danger, it failed in its duty to the airline. The airline had a right to rely on the overhauler's performance. Thus, it could recover from the overhauler for loss of the aircraft, together with reimbursement for compensation paid to survivors of the four passengers.

In a North Carolina case a twin engine Beechcraft was delivered to the Municipal Airport terminal and service facility about noon on a July day. The pilot went to a radio repair shop to arrange for some needed radio repair, after which he left the airport for a visit to Charlotte. While he was away a storm arose with heavy rain and wind. Upon returning to the airport he saw the aircraft wedged between a tree and a telephone pole 150 feet south of where he had parked it. Gusts from the storm had reached 92 mph.

In a suit by the aircraft owner against the repair facility, the judge found that the facility had accepted the aircraft for the purpose of checking and repairing the radios and, thus, had possession and control of the aircraft; that it had adequate warning of the approaching storm; that it had negligently failed to secure the aircraft against the expected damaging weather conditions.

The facility representative argued that the damage was caused by "an act of God" rather than by negligence of the facility. The judge rejected this argument on the grounds that the damage could have been avoided by the facility's exercise of reasonable care

and foresight. Thus, the facility was
liable for damage to the aircraft.

FLIGHT SCHOOL OPERATION

A flight school operator owes a high duty of care to
its student pilots; it assumes the contractual duty
of giving the student an adequate course of training
using competent instructors and suitable aircraft.
The school operator will probably be liable to the
student and any other persons injured by the
student pilot if the operator permits the student to
fly solo with insufficient training, thereby leading
to an accident.

It must be borne in mind that a pilot trainee must
exercise reasonable care for his own welfare as
well as that of others. Such things as his previous
training, total flight time and the surrounding
circumstrances will be considered in retrospect if
the question of the trainee's contributory fault
arises.

In a Louisiana case an injured student had held his
private pilot's license for eleven months at the time
of the accident, and had a total flight time of 112
hours. He had flown solo to other cities inside and
outside Louisiana and was receiving further
instruction toward his commercial license. On the
day of the accident his regular instructor was not
available. The student was asked if he would fly
with the president of the school serving as
instructor. He agreed to do so. Several flight
maneuvers in the Stearman aircraft were
demonstrated by the instructor. After four or five
regular landings by the student, the president took
over the controls and told the student to throttle
back at any time he chose, this being for the
purpose of demonstrating the forced-landing-
after-takeoff technique. When the aircraft was at
a 300-foot altitude, the student closed the
throttle. The instructor attempted a 90-degree turn
to the left, stalled, did not add power to recover
and the crash resulted. In a suit against the

school operator the student was awarded money damages for personal injuries, loss of wages and medical expenses.

Other discussion applicable to Flight Schools is covered under FIXED BASE OPERATOR, AIRCRAFT and INSURANCE.

POSSESSION OF ANOTHER'S AIRCRAFT

Aircraft loss or damage often occurs while a person other than the owner has possession. Some examples are:

1.   Damage by windstorm to aircraft while tied down;

2.   Damage or loss by fire while the aircraft is stored;

3.   Loss by theft while the aircraft is stored;

4.   Damage or loss due to an accident while the aircraft is being flown by a pilot other than the owner.

Whenever a person other than the owner has legal possession of an aircraft, he has a legal duty to exercise a reasonable degree of care for the protection and preservation of the aircraft. This degree of care is higher in certain circumstances than in others; it will be determined by such things as whether the person in possession has been paid a fee or is merely acting gratuitously as custodian for the benefit of the owner.   Further, an agreement between the owner and the possessor relating to storage or operation will also be considered in determining the degree of care required, whether there has been a failure to exercise such care, and who must bear the loss.

> In a California case a party of five
> fishermen boarded a rented aircraft
> licensed to carry only four passengers.
> In attempting to land at a runway that

40

was too short, the aircraft ended up on its back with a salvage value of $300. All five passengers were found to be joint venturers; they were all equally liable for acts and negligence of each other, including poor judgment exercised by the pilot. The owner of the aircraft was entitled to recover the reasonable market value of the aircraft based on its value immediately prior to the crash, less the $300 of salvage value.

A procedural problem that occasionally arises relates to the question of whether the owner or the one in possession has the burden of proof if an aircraft is damaged. That is, should the aircraft owner be required to prove the possessor did not exercise proper care, or, should the possessor be required to prove he did exercise proper care.

It is important to keep in mind that mere possession of another's aircraft does not necessarily make the possessor an insurer against any and all damage. Thus, each case must be evaluated on the basis of the particular fact situation and the applicable state law.

AIRPORT OWNERSHIP OR OPERATION

Due to the nature of airport operation, the owners and operators are exposed to liability from activities that are directly, as well as indirectly, related to aircraft. Activities directly related include aircraft operation, fuel and oil servicing, aircraft storage, maintenance and repair, ramp service, rescue and fire fighting. Associated indirect activities and conditions include operation of automobile parking lots, elevators and escalators, special entertainment events, restaurant and food service, and maintenance of areas such as hallways and stairways. Persons to whom a duty is owed may include airplane owners, passengers, concessionaires or lessees, spectators, visitors and restaurant patrons.

Most of the larger airports are operated by some governmental organization or agency, such as a city, county or port authority. Generally, in most states, since this is a form of business enterprise, the rules pertaining to liability of these operators are the same as for private operators. There is an obligation to see that the airport premises are safe for such persons as are entitled to use them and to give an appropriate warning of any danger or hazard of which the proprietor knows or should know, and of which the visitor does not know or may not reasonably be deemed to know. This includes keeping the runways free from obstructions, and placing markers warning of any hazard. The operator may also be liable for damage or destruction of aircraft tied down or stored on the airport premises. This is discussed further under POSSESSION OF ANOTHER'S AIRCRAFT and FIXED BASE OPERATOR.

In a Florida case an aircraft undergoing overhaul in one of the airport hangars was destroyed by fire. The port authority which operated the airport was required to pay for the loss of the aircraft. Evidence introduced at the trial indicated the operator was negligent in: (1) failing to provide fire fighting equipment, (2) failing to provide a fire alarm system, (3) allowing a renter of the hangar to create an unusual and additional fire hazard by storing a large number of airplane engines in wooden crates in the hangar, and (4) by permitting fuel tanks to be drained inside the hangar.

In a California case a pilot was injured and his aircraft damaged during a landing and attempted go-around when the wheels of his aircraft struck a mound of dirt running along the shoulder of the runway. The airport operator was held liable since the mound had become obscured by weeds in such a way the pilot was not aware of its existence.

In an Oregon case an aircraft was
destroyed by high winds after it had
been left tied down on the airport
premises. The airport operator had
used worn and frayed tie-down lines
even though he had knowledge of an
approaching storm and the probability
of winds much stronger than normal.
The jury found that the airport operator
had legal possession of the aircraft
rather than merely renting tie-down
space to the aircraft owner. Thus, he
was liable for the loss since he should
have exercised greater care to prevent
it.

It is noteworthy that a few states grant to a
governmental agency operating an airport a degree
of immunity from suit. This is on the theory that
operation of the airport is a "governmental"
function rather than a business or proprietary
function. This is discussed further under
GOVERNMENT LIABILITY.

FLYING CLUBS

Although there are many practical concerns
associated with formation and operation of flying
clubs, the principal legal problems concern (1)
aircraft ownership, (2) aircraft operation and (3)
insurance coverage.

The basis of a flying club is an agreement, formal or
informal, written or oral, that certain persons
will conduct a joint undertaking for their mutual
benefit. If the club is incorporated, the Articles
of Incorporation, bylaws and operating rules make
up the agreement.

OWNERSHIP OF FLYING CLUB AIRCRAFT

Transfer of title from individuals or corporations to
a non-profit corporation organized for purposes of

the club is one way of owning club aircraft. Joint ownership by individuals is another. An additional frequent practice is that of leasing aircraft from an individual owner for use by the club members. The owner can be a club member or someone not associated with the club.

LIABILITY OF FLYING CLUB MEMBERS

If the club is incorporated, an individual member is not by virtue of membership alone personally liable for accidents of other members; the corporation is liable for accidents of its members and its assets may be sold to satisfy any judgment against it if there is insufficient liability insurance coverage. A member may be liable, however, for his own negligence while flying the club aircraft. For this reason it is imperative each member have adequate liability insurance through a club group policy or an individual policy. Additional non-owner policies can be purchased by individuals who fly aircraft owned by flying clubs. This may be advisable if the club policy limits are not high enough to satisfy needs of the individual pilot.

INTEREST OF CLUB MEMBER

If the club is incorporated, an individual member owns an intangible proportionate membership interest in the club assets; he does not own a specific interest in any given aircraft or other property of the club. If the club is not incorporated, the member may own a proportionate joint interest in aircraft or other club property. In any event, the right to sell or transfer an individual interest is controlled by the membership agreement under which the club is formed and operated. If there is no express membership agreement the law of the particular state will imply an agreement in keeping with the relationship of co-owners, joint venturers or partners.

QUASI FLYING CLUB

A considerable number of business operators have established special rental programs referred to as

"Flying Clubs". These are promotional programs designed to attract persons who wish to rent aircraft at rates somewhat lower than those available to casual or occasional renters. Usually a small initiation charge is paid to qualify as a "member". The status of the member is that of a renter-pilot when flying an aircraft owned by this type of business operator. The member owns no interest in the aircraft or the business, and is subject to liability as an individual. Before engaging in this type of flying activity a pilot should assure himself of that the operator's policy covers the pilot's liability for damage to the aircraft as well as liability to persons who might be injured or killed by the aircraft.

TITLE SEARCH BEFORE PURCHASE OF CLUB AIRCRAFT

In addition to the many practical factors that must be considered prior to purchase of an aircraft, there should be a TITLE SEARCH of records filed with the FAA's Aircraft Registry Office in Oklahoma City to assure a clear title free of liens and encumbrances. If the purchase is to be financed by a lending institution, the lender will usually conduct its own title search. This subject is discussed further under the section on AIRCRAFT PURCHASE, SALE, TITLE RECORDING.

CLUB INSURANCE

Acquisition of appropriate insurance is a major challenge for flying clubs. Very few club members have any substantial knowledge of aircraft insurance or how to go about securing appropriate coverage. Moreover there is a dearth of competent professional advisors readily available to provide guidance.

If the club is incorporated and has no liability insurance, or has inadequate coverage, assets of the corporation are subject to sale for payment of any judgment rendered against the club. If the club is not incorporated, assets of individual members would be subject to sale in this type of situation. This could include assets owned by members other than the pilot flying at the time of an accident in which liability is incurred.

The type and amount of insurance that should be carried by the club may vary from one state to another. State requirements are usually lower than is desirable from a practical point of view. Generally, it should cover bodily injury and property damage, including injury or death of any passengers that are to be carried. Hull insurance on the club aircraft will likely be required by any lending institution providing financing. If the club owns the aircraft outright, hull coverage is optional.

PASSENGERS' RIGHTS

Understandably, with the vast number of persons utilizing general aviation and airline aircraft as a means of transportation, many fact situations arise with legal implications respecting passenger rights. Generally, the problems fall into such categories as injury or death while aboard the aircraft, injury while boarding or deplaning, lost or damaged luggage, delays or missed airline connections, embarrassment and humiliation, unreasonable discrimination, and insurance coverage.

A passenger's rights will be affected by such things as whether he is traveling aboard an aircraft of an airline, a charter operator, an air taxi operator or merely a private aircraft; whether he had paid a fare or is merely a gratuitous guest. An airline operator, a charter operator or an air taxi operator is required to exercise the highest degree of care for the safety of its passengers. The pilot or owner of a private aircraft has a somewhat lesser duty to a passenger who has paid nothing for passage, but may nevertheless be liable for any injury.

Additionally, a number of states have enacted "guest statutes". Certain states have repealed these statutes. In states still having guest statutes a person accepting a ride in an aircraft, giving nothing in exchange, must bear the loss resulting from any negligent conduct of his pilot host. In this situation, only if the injured guest or his heirs can prove the host pilot was intoxicated or had brought about injury or death through willful misconduct can there be any recovery of compensation irrespective of liability insurance coverage carried by the host pilot at the time of the accident. Certain states also specify "gross negligence" as a basis for recovery.

In states having guest statutes many well-meaning private and commercial pilots offering courtesy rides do not realize they are subjecting their friends and acquaintances to risk of injury or death which would not be covered by insurance. Rarely, of course, does the passenger have any awareness of this lack of insurance coverage. Generally, these laws are copied from similar automobile guest statutes, the latter having been enacted to discourage "litigious hitchhikers" -- a concept generally considered not suited to aviation.

> In a Virginia case a fixed base operator was conducting free demonstation flights as part of a promotional program. During one ten-minute flight, a short series of mild aerobatics was performed. One of his passengers, a 16 year old girl, became dizzy, excited and upset. After landing, the girl left the airplane without any aid, direction or warning from the pilot and was struck by the aircraft propeller, receiving serious injuries. The jury decided the pilot had failed to exercise reasonable care in not warning the girl of the danger from the propeller and not directing her to a place of safety. The operator of the flying service was liable for the girl's injuries even though she had paid nothing for the flight.

"PASS" PASSENGERS -- WAIVER OF RIGHTS

An additional problem which may limit or preclude recovery against an airline is presented by the printed waiver often included on the ticket issued by an airline to certain passengers accorded "pass" privileges. This is prevalent among airline employees and their families when riding the aircraft of their own airline or of another airline under a reciprocal pass arrangement. In theory, the passenger "assumes the risk" of any injury; in reality, many such passengers are not aware of this waiver of their rights. The waiver would not relieve other persons or organizations, such as the U.S. Government or the aircraft manufacturer, who may have contributed to causation of an airline accident.

AIRCRAFT MANUFACTURERS' LIABILITY

During recent years, there has been a trend by the courts to place greater responsibility on manufacturers with respect to defects in aircraft or their component parts. In many states the traditional legal theories of negligence and contract have been modified with adoption of the theory of "absolute" or "strict" liability imposing a much higher duty of care on the manufacturer. This duty extends not only to the purchaser of the aircraft, but also to the pilot, passengers riding in the aircraft and persons on the ground who are injured or have their property damaged as a result of a defect in the aircraft.

A manufacturer may be held liable also for failure to adequately instruct a purchaser in the proper operational technique, or to inform him of an aircraft's known dangerous characteristics.

A rationale for imposing broad liability on the manufacturer is the ability, through liability insurance or otherwise, to bear the expense of personal injury or loss, as opposed to the individual financial burden which would be placed on the injured person, or the burden on society in having to care for an injured individual unable to care for himself. Likewise survivors should receive compensation for that lost by virtue of death of the deceased.

In a New Jersey case an aircraft crashed following an engine overspeed after the pilot was unable to feather the propeller. In a suit brought by personal representatives of deceased passengers, the manufacturer was held to be under a continuing duty after sale to develop and improve its existing propeller systems. This continuing duty extended to passengers in an aircraft since it was foreseeable they might be injured if a propeller were defective.

In an early and rather unusual North Carolina case, based on the crash in California of a Gyroglider, the manufacturer was held not responsible for the pilot's injuries. After having personally assembled the Gyroglider, the pilot had made two successful flights, with the third being a disastrous dive from an altitude of approximately 100 feet. The pilot brought suit against the manufacturer based on advertisements published in North Carolina to the effect that purchasers "could use the aircraft in complete safety". In applying the North Carolina law the Court found the manufacturer not liable since there was no "privity" between the pilot and the manufacturer. The aircraft had been purchased by the pilot from a third party dealer rather than directly from the manufacturer.

This North Carolina court decision represents a result typical of earlier cases involving defective products, including aircraft. Although North

Carolina still followed the older "privity" requirement rule, if the pilot had been able to bring suit in California, he probably would have prevailed against the manufacturer since California has abrogated the privity requirement and favors the person injured.

This case again points out the importance of understanding the laws of the particular state or states where a given flight is conducted, and that a given set of facts might lead to different results in different states.

U. S. GOVERNMENT LIABILITY

Under the common-law system as it was inherited from England, the government could not be sued without its consent. This followed from the ancient theory, "The King can do no wrong". Although certain vestiges of this concept are still with us today, many exceptions have been provided by Congress and individual state legislatures. Generally, suit against the Government will not be entertained if based on acts discretionary or governmental in nature, as opposed to those ministerial or commercial in nature.

A local government--be it state, county, city or a governmental agency--may be held liable for its negligent acts arising from its responsibilities as a commercial airport owner or operator.

Insofar as the United States federal government is concerned, it too can be held liable for negligence. The Federal Tort Claims Act is the legislative consent basis for liability in many aviation cases where Government aircraft or employees are involved. Liability may stem from control exercised by the government in various phases of civil aviation, such as air route and tower traffic control. The Act provides that all such cases are to be tried by a federal judge sitting without a jury. Claims against the United States may be based on damage or loss of property, or for personal injury or death caused by the negligent acts or omissions of federal employees who are acting within the scope of their employment at the time of the accident.

Frequently, the federal government and the private operator of an aircraft are jointly liable for an accident, such as a mid-air collison where air traffic control is a factor.

One of the basic functions of an air traffic controller or tower operator is to provide separation between aircraft. Another is to provide significant weather information. There is very limited or no duty, however, to determine the qualifications of a pilot to follow clearances for the type of flight requested. Likewise, there is very limited or no duty to determine that an aircraft has suitable equipment for the type of flight anticipated, or for the type of instrument approach requested.

The Government has not assumed and will not assume the responsibility for all aircraft accidents. But the United States has been held liable in several cases where air traffic controllers failed to consider weather conditions in their clearance operations. Any significant change in weather relating to an instrument approach should be reported by a tower operator to an approaching pilot. This is in keeping with the heavy degree of reliance those who fly place upon the Government for assistance.

> In an early precedent-setting case a chartered aircraft returning the California State Polytechnic College football team to Santa Maria, California, from Toledo, Ohio, crashed during takeoff from the Toledo Express Airport. The weather at the time of the crash was zero ceiling and zero visibility. The tower controllers were held to have been negligent in their duty to the passengers by failing to deny takeoff clearnace to the pilot, and in

failing to warn him not to take off and
that if he did take off he would be
violating a Federal Aviation Regulation. The court said the controllers
knowingly assisted the pilot in violating
a Federal Aviation Regulation which
prohibited the takeoff when visibility
was below prescribed minimums, and
which was enacted to protect
passengers.

In a case involving the crash on takeoff
at the Honolulu, Hawaii, airport of a
Piper PA-18, the U. S. Government was
held liable on the basis of negligence of
the control tower operator. The Piper
had been cleared for takeoff
immediately following the takeoff on a
cross-runway of a DC-8. After being
caught in turbulence of the departing
jet, the Piper crashed killing the
student and his instructor. The
student's heirs were allowed to recover;
those of the instructor were not since
the instructor had not exercised
reasonable care for his own safety.

AIRLINES' LIABILITY TO PASSENGERS AND OTHERS

The ticket purchased from a travel agent or from an
airline constitutes a contractual agreement
between the purchaser and the airline relating to
the passenger and his luggage. Implied in this
contract is the airline's obligation to fly the
passenger in a safe manner and to use reasonable
care respecting his luggage. If an item of
luggage is of exceptional value or requires
special handling, this fact should be brought to the
attention of appropriate airline agents before the
luggage is loaded aboard the aircraft.
Otherwise, the airline will likely not be liable for
its full value if it is lost or damaged, but will be
liable for no more than $750 even though the actual
value is higher.

An airline may be held contractually liable if injury or death occurs, but liability does not extend to failure to operate according to schedule, or to delays of a common nature, or for failure to meet a passenger's connecting flight.

A passenger with a reserved seat who is involuntarily denied boarding on an oversold flight may be entitled to compensation. The amount may vary, based on value of the remaining flight coupons up to the next stopover, and any alternate transportation available.

No compensation for denied boarding will be given, however, if (a) the passenger does not comply with the carrier's requirements as to reservation reconfirmation, ticketing, check-in, etc.; (b) there is inadequate seating space due to government requisition; or (c) substitution of aircraft of lesser capacity due to operational or safety reasons is required.

An airline is also subject to the law of negligence. It will be held responsible for injury, death or property damage resulting from its failure to exercise a high degree of care for safety of its passengers and their property. Violation by a company of its own operating rules may be evidence of negligence since these usually set forth the requisite standard of conduct. Failure to inspect and maintain the aircraft in airworthy condition is also a basis for liability if this leads to an accident.

It must be borne in mind the airline may invoke the defenses of "contributory fault" or "assumption of risk" if an injured passenger has failed to exercise reasonable care for his own safety.

For example, if a passenger fails to utilize his seat belt after being warned of probable turbulent air conditions, he will likely have to bear his own loss if turbulence is encountered and he is injured.

An incident occurred in Texas as a four-

engine turbo-prop aircraft commenced
its takeoff from the Greater Southwest
Airport near Fort Worth. As the plane
sped along the runway and was about to
become airborne, the captain's seat
unexpectedly slid backwards projecting
him away from the instrument panel and
the controls. This prompted the
captain to abort the takeoff. The
deceleration was so abrupt it threw the
passengers against their seat belts and
one man was injured. The court agreed
that the airline was negligent in its
failure to inspect and maintain the
pilot's seat, and that this negligence
was the legal cause of the passenger's
injury.

According to the Federal Aviation Act of 1958 an
airline must not subject a passenger to any "undue"
or "unreasonable" discrimination or disadvantage.
This does not mean, however, that all passengers
must be treated exactly the same in every respect.
Such treatment would not be feasible due to the
nature of airline operations.

A Los Angeles attorney desired to make
a business trip to Louisville, Kentucky,
and reserved round trip tourist space.
On the evening before his return flight,
he advised the airline's agent of his
intention to utilize his reservation.
Upon arrival at the airport an hour
before the scheduled departure for Los
Angeles, the lawyer was advised that
the flight had been oversold and that he
had been placed on standby. He was
refused permission to board the flight.
He brought suit against the airline
contending that he was unduly
prejudiced and that unreasonable
preference was given to others in
violation of the law in that at least
seven first-class passengers who were
carried in the tourist section of the

aircraft had made reservations after his had been confirmed.

The judge held that the attorney was entitled to priority in flight accommodations over all other passengers who had made reservations later than he and who were permitted to board the flight. The judge further held that by disregarding the attorney's priority, the airline unjustly and unreasonably discriminated against him. He was awarded out-of-pocket compensatory damages of $1.54 -- the cost of the telephone call made to his wife in Los Angeles to explain his delayed arrival -- and $5,000 exemplary or punitive damages as vindication of his rights as a passenger, and to impress the airline with the need to protect the rights of every air passenger from future unreasonable treatment. A factor influencing the judge in allowing the $5,000 award was the fact that oversales by the airline had averaged 2,000 seats a month, and that nearly 700 passengers had to be removed from domestic flights each month during a six-month period.

Additional bases for possible airline liability are accidents occurring on airport terminal premises such as waiting areas or walkways that are under control of a particular airline.

Further discussion of this subject is included in the sections on PASSENGERS' RIGHTS and AIRPORT OWNERS AND OPERATORS.

MILITARY LIABILITY

Military aircraft frequently are involved in crashes or other incidents which cause damage to property, injury or death. Recovery against the United States Government for military pilot negligence is provided for by the Federal Tort Claims Act. Military aircraft are generally required to operate in accordance with Federal Aviation Regulations when operating within civilian airspace. Deviation is permissible with prior approval.

In an early South Carolina case a farmer was mowing his pasture with a mowing machine towed by a team of two mules. He stopped his team to cool off in the shade of a pine tree. While kneeling behind the mowing blade and oiling it, he heard a severe penetrating noise which grew louder as it approached. Glancing behind him he saw an Army helicopter flying directly toward him at tree-top level. He grabbed the reins of his team to keep them from bolting. The helicopter continued to fly toward him and passed overhead at a height of some 35 to 40 feet, at which time the mules lurched forward. The farmer's right leg was almost amputated by the mowing blade. Whether or not the United States was liable for actionable negligence had to be determined by the laws of South Carolina since the Federal Tort Claims Act provides that the United States shall be liable if a private person would be liable in accordance with the law of the place where the accident occurred. The judge stated it was common knowledge that livestock in general, and mules in particular, are easily frightened by sudden loud noises and by objects which are propelled directly at or over their heads. The farmer and his team of mules were in plain sight in the pasture when the helicopter, making a loud noise, was flown directly over their heads. It was reasonably foreseeable by the pilot that the team would bolt. The operation of the aircraft in such a manner constituted actionable negligence. A

> $25,000 judgment against the United
> States was ordered.

Additional discussion of this subject is included in
the sections on SONIC BOOM and U. S.
GOVERNMENT LIABILITY.

MILITARY PILOT'S INJURY OR DEATH

Although an injured military pilot cannot sue the
government for his injuries, he may be able to hold
the aircraft manufacturer liable if the aircraft was
defectively manufactured or designed. Likewise
he would be able to hold a civilian operator liable
for causing an accident. This principle applies to
the pilot's heirs if the pilot is killed as a result of
such a defect.

> In a New York case the heirs of an Air
> Force pilot were allowed to recover
> compensation from the engine manufac-
> turer after engine failure caused a fatal
> crash of a military aircraft. Except as
> against the U. S. Government, the rights
> of a military pilot and his survivors are
> equivalent to those of a civilian pilot in
> this respect.

"MOONLIGHTING" PILOTS

Airline pilots and others having a primary employer
often engage in other flying activities such as
flight instruction or charter operation.
Compensation for the pilot's services may be in
money, use of aircraft or some other form. Certain
possible adverse legal consequences should be
considered before undertaking these activities:

1. The pilot's Workers' Compensation Insurance
provided in connection with his regular employment
will likely not be in effect during this period;

2. His accident and sickness insurance will
probably not be in effect during this period;

3.   He may incur personal liability for damage to
the aircraft he is flying;

4.   He may incur personal liability for injury or
death of passengers resulting from an accident;

5.   He may incur personal liability for damage to
another's property;

6.   If he is an airline pilot, the Air Line Pilot's
Association will not furnish legal assistance in
defense of any FAA charge arising during this
period;

7.   The pilot may be in violation of contract with
his primary employer, thus, leading to disciplinary
action or discharge;

8.   Flight hours should be monitored so as not to
exceed applicable FAR limits for a particular
period.

It is noteworthy that certain primary employers are
amenable to continued Workers' Compensation
Insurance coverage while a pilot-employee is
employed elsewhere. A pilot contemplating such
employment would be well advised to investigate
this possibility before undertaking outside activity.

Before undertaking any type of flying activities, a
pilot should assure himself of adequate personal
liability insurance coverage. Additionally, any
aircraft he is flying should be covered for loss or
damage for the particular type of operation. If
the aircraft is not properly insured the pilot could
end up paying out of his pocket for any damage
occuring while he has possession.

AIRCRAFT INSURANCE

Two major principles relating to aircraft insurance
must be borne in mind: (1) Insurance functions as
compensation for loss; this loss must be

substantiated by proof of both nature and extent before an insurance underwriter is obligated to make payment; (2) Insurance coverage is provided as a profit-making business undertaking. Thus, good business practices dictate that claims be denied unless there is a strong probability the insurance company is legally liable under the policy in question. Moreover, a claims adjusting agent is duty bound to his employer, the underwriter, to settle claims for the minimum amount acceptable to the claimant.

Some of the more common types of insurance coverage that are of interest to pilots and aircraft owners relate to:

1. Loss of own life

2. Physical injury to self

3. Medical and hospital expenses for self and others

4. Liability for injury or death of others

5. Liability for damage to property of others

6. Damage to or loss of aircraft being flown

7. Loss of income for periods of physical disability, and

8. Workers' Compensation relating to employment related injuries

UNCERTAINTY OF POLICY COVERAGE

Although great sums of money are paid out yearly as insurance premiums, rarely does an individual pilot, aircraft owner or business operator know the full extent or nature of the coverage--or lack of coverage--for which he is paying. This is due partly to vague or ambiguous clauses and phrases contained in the individual policies. A second reason is a general lack of interest in the subject of insurance. A related third reason is a lack of appreciation for the importance played by insurance. This frequently results in failure of the insured to read that portion of the policy which is clear.

In theory, an insurance policy represents a written memorandum of contractual agreement between the insured and the insurer. In reality, this is seldom true since the individual insured does not know the legal or practical effects of the policy. Under group policy coverage an additional obscuring factor exists due to lack of contact between the individual insured and the insurance agent or broker who is responsible for providing the policy.

UNCLEAR POLICY TERMS

An insurance company will not make payment without strong indication it is legally required to do so; thus, many court cases have been required to determine the meaning of such words and phrases as "engage in", "participate in", "as a result of", "navigation", "crew", "duties relating to aircraft", "flight", "officer or other member of crew", "in consequence of", "riding in", "scheduled air carrier", "student pilot", and "powered aircraft". Since such phrases are interpreted in conjunction with other clauses and provisions of the policy, a particular phrase may have different meanings when used in different policies.

COURT EXAMPLES

When required to interpret certain given aircraft insurance policies courts have reached such conclusions as in the following examples:

1. Interpreted the word "passenger" as not including a student pilot;

2. The words "as a passenger" were held to mean "as an occupant", thus, allowing recovery for death of the pilot of a plane which crashed;

3.   Use of an aircraft in an airshow was held to be a "business use";

4.   The term "student pilot" did not include a pilot previously licensed as a private pilot and who was taking additional instruction in order to qualify for a commercial certificate;

5.   The term "passengers" in reference to persons carried by a student pilot referred to guest occupants as well as fare paying passengers;

6.   Exclusion of "any aviation sales or service or repair organization" did not apply to the business of selling aircraft supplies and equipment;

7.   Unauthorized meddling with an aircraft resulting in its movement and collision with a hangar was not within the policy coverage relating to "use";

8.   An exclusionary clause relating to "violation of FAA airworthiness or pilot certificates" did not include operation by an intoxicated pilot;

9.   Exclusionary clause for "violations of FAA regulations" did not apply even though a non-instrument trained pilot inadvertently flew into clouds;

10. Operation of an airplane overloaded by 80 pounds was not in violation of FAA regulations pertaining to "airworthiness certificate";

11. Recovery of compensation was not allowed for loss of a helicopter when it was being operated by a pilot other than those pilots "named and approved" in the policy;

12. Recovery was not allowed where aircraft not specifically listed in the policy crashed injuring passengers;

13. "License" requirements of the insurance policy did not include by implication federal regulations requirement of current "medical certificate".

COURT RULES OF POLICY INTERPRETATION

Certain general court rules of construction and interpretation of policies are worth noting:

1. Words particularly applicable to the insurance business will be given their usual interpretation;

2. An insurance policy will be read as a whole in an attempt to determine the intention of the parties;

3. Words will be given their ordinary meaning if they are not recognized words particularly applicable to the insurance business;

4. Where an ambiguity still exists, the policy will be construed in favor of the insured rather than the insurer since the latter had the choice of words in drafting the policy;

5. If a later executed, typewritten provision conflicts with an earlier printed provision, the typewritten provision will prevail;

6. If a rider provision conflicts with a provision of the policy itself, the rider will prevail;

7. In certain states operation of an aircraft in violation of an exclusionary clause of the policy will not affect coverage if there is no connection between that clause and an accident; in other states the policy is deemed to be void during any period in which any violation is in effect.

AMBIGUOUS PROVISIONS AFFECTING POLICY COVERAGE

Most insurance policies contain numerous ambiguous exclusions, conditions, clauses and and provisions limiting the insurance company's liability. The individual insured pilot, aircraft owner or business operator would be well advised to secure written clarifying information prior to loss regarding any provision of the policy which is not clear.

Although this may not be easy to accomplish, securing the information in writing will tend to preclude any need for court action in that respect if a loss is subsequently experienced. Complying with this request will impose a slight amount of additional work on the insurance company's service agent. He may be willing to secure the information requested only if he is in danger of losing a client for failure to do so. In fairness to smaller independent agents, some of them do not have sufficient influence or "clout" to persuade their underwriters that this information should be given to the insured. The agent's oral interpretations of the policy should not be relied on. If the agent attempts to dismiss the request for clarifying information using terminology such as "standard policy" or "usual coverage", he is skirting the request by being noncommital in a nonbinding manner. Persistence by the insured will be required to assure compliance with the request.

APPLICATION FORM

Since an insurance policy is a memorandum of contractual agreement, certain information is required by the insurance company before there can be the requisite legal "meetings of the minds" between the company and the applicant. There are basically three questions decided by the company from information contained in the application form:

1. Should insurance coverage be issued to the applicant?

2. What amount and what type of coverage should be issued?

3. What amount of premium should be charged for this coverage?

It is of great importance that the applicant provide accurate information sought by the application form; otherwise, any insurance policy issued may be void or voidable at the insurance company's option.

Although an insignificant inaccuracy in the application form might not render a policy void or voidable, the distinction between "insignificant" and "significant" inaccuracies is not always easy to determine. When requested, information should be provided in respect to such matters as age of applicant, total number of flight hours as pilot, past medical treatment, and type of flight in which the applicant will be engaged. This information is used by the insurance representative to evaluate the risk being assumed and to determine the appropriate premium for to be charged for that risk.

WAIVER OF BENEFITS

Following submission of an application for insurance coverage, an applicant may be requested by the insurance company to waive rights to coverage of certain provisions in a printed policy. This may be based on such things as the applicant's medical history or certain type of flight operations anticipated. Since this is a limitation on the company's liability, it is important the pilot understand the scope and extent of the particular waiver. Further, in theory, since the insurance company is assuming a lesser risk, the premium for this coverage should be adjusted accordingly.

LIFE AND ACCIDENT INSURANCE

Although not technically characterized as "aircraft insurance" many traditional, non-aviation insurance policies covering death, disability or medical benefits contain exclusionary "aviation clauses". These clauses are designed to limit the insurer's liability in respect to certain aviation activities, such as death occurring while riding in or piloting an aircraft. Whenever a claim is made on one of these policies, two troublesome questions may be presented: (1) What is the meaning of this clause? (2) Was the status of the insured such as to bring him within the exclusion of this clause? Evaluation of the particular fact situation is required to answer these questions.

AIRCRAFT HULL INSURANCE

Aircraft hull insurance can be written to cover physical loss or damage to the insured aircraft while it is on the ground and not moving under its own power, or to cover all risks to the insured aircraft except while in flight, or to cover the insured aircraft for all risks both on the ground and in flight.

In a considerable number of cases it has been necessary to determine whether the insured aircraft was or was not in flight at the time of loss or damage. Certain policies define the phrase "in flight" as embracing "the period from the time the aircraft moves forward in taking off, or in attempting to take off for air transit, while in the air, and until the aircraft completes its landing and landing run after contact with the land or water".

Suit against the insurance company is frequently required to determine whether hull coverage applies to a given accident.

> In a New York case recovery was sought under a "ground risks" clause of a policy after an aircraft had crashed into the ocean. The court allowed recovery for damage resulting from unsuccessful efforts to salvage the craft and that resulting from salt water since these occurred subsequent to the crash. Recovery was not allowed, however, for the damage caused by impact since that was considered damage occurring while the aircraft was in flight.

> In a Massachusetts case an aircraft was damaged when it ran beyond the landing strip and upset because of defective brakes. The court found this to be a "flight loss" rather than a "taxiing loss" since the speed of the aircraft had not been reduced to normal taxiing

speed prior to impact.

In a Mississippi case a gust of wind capsized a plane after the pilot had landed and reduced the speed to five or ten miles an hour. The court found the loss to be within coverage relating to "all risks basis while not in flight".

Fire and collision damage to aircraft have presented problems of policy interpretation. In a New York case suit was brought on a policy insuring against "fire and explosion arising while the aircraft is not in flight". The subject plane was destroyed by fire which was first observed about the engine within two minutes after it had overturned. It had rolled 30 to 50 feet in the making of a forced landing on a snow covered field due to engine trouble. The court held that the loss resulted from a fire arising while the airplane was "in flight", thus, it was not within coverage of the policy.

In a New Jersey case suit was brought upon a policy covering a seaplane. The policy provided indemnity for damage to the craft caused by "collision with the earth (including land or water) or any object moving or stationary". Upon experiencing mechanical difficulties, the pilot had successfully landed the aircraft on an open sea, after which it drifted upon the beach and was substantially damaged by action of the waves. The court held that such damage resulted from "collision" as the term was used within the policy.

In a Louisiana case an aircraft caught in the wake turbulence of another aircraft made a forced landing and began burning shortly thereafter. The subject fire

insurance policy was held to apply to
fires only, and not to fires caused by or
resulting from collision or crash of the
aircraft. Thus, the insurance company
did not have to pay for the damage.

UNLAWFUL OR IMPROPER USE OF INSURED AIRCRAFT

Policies often contain exclusionary clauses relating
to damage or loss from particular enumerated types
of operation. Insurance companies have been
relieved of liability for loss or damage to aircraft
based on such exclusionary clauses as the
following:

1. Operation of an aircraft in violation of Federal
Aviation Regulations;

2. Operation in any type of flying which requires a
waiver by the Federal Aviation Administration;

3. Operation of an aircraft by a pilot other than
that named in the policy;

4. Operation by pilots not having the requisite
certificates or ratings;

5. Use of an aircraft for instruction purposes;

6. Operation by a pilot not having the specified
minimum amount of flying time;

7. Operation by pilots not approved for schedule;

8. Operation of aircraft by student pilots;

9. Operation of a flight for which payment is
received;

10. Operation under instrument flight conditions;

11. Loss due to theft.

LIABILITY INSURANCE

Aviation liability insurance may be written to cover

civil liability of an aircraft owner, an individual
pilot or a business operator. It normally covers
losses due to injury, death or property damage
caused by an aircraft accident. The insured is
protected for liability imposed upon him by law for
negligent acts or omission; there is no coverage
for intentional wrongful acts. If the act in
question is in violation of state or federal law it is
usually excluded as no being within the risk
assumed by the insurance company.

Liability of a pilot, the aircraft owner or business
operator for injury or death to passengers, or
persons on the ground may be determined by
applying the law of the state where an accident
occurs, where the aircraft is normally based or
where the business operator has its place of
business.

A number of states have enacted "guest statutes"
for application to aircraft accident losses. These
statutes have limited civil liability to such
situations as accidents resulting from the pilot's
intoxication, willful misconduct or gross negligence
if the guest has not given payment for his passage.
In states having these "guest statutes" many well-
meaning pilots and aircraft owners extend courtesy
rides to friends and associates not realizing they
are being subjected to risks for which there is no
insurance coverage.

As with other forms of insurance, rarely does the
insured aircraft owner or pilot have other than a
vague notion of the scope or extent of liability
insurance coverage he has received in exchange for
the premium he has paid. Much disappointment,
delay and expense result from attempts to collect
on these policies, when, following an accident, an
insurance company adjuster states, "But that is not
covered."

**STATEMENT TO INSURANCE INVESTIGATING
AGENT - CAUTION !**

Shortly following an accident in which a passenger

or crew member is injured, an investigation will be made by an agent of the appropriate insurance company. This investigation is primarily for the purpose of gaining information favorable to the insurance company. Typically, a hospital visit will be made to secure a statement of an injured person. Since there is no obligation to make an immediate statement, the injured person would be well advised to defer making any statement until he has recovered from any medication or emotional upset. Legal advice should be sought before making any statement. Reason: Any statement by the injured person may later be used against him as a basis for denying or limiting insurance coverage, or as a basis for imposing civil liability in a later suit. This is particularly applicable to statements of nature and extent of injuries, details of the accident and statements as to cause of the accident.

WORKERS' COMPENSATION INSURANCE

Under our common law system inherited from England, a master or employer was responsible for providing his servant or employee with a safe place to work; a place where the employee would be protected from dangers which the employer might be expected to have known about, anticipated or discovered. The employer also had a duty to provide safe tools, appliances and equipment for the work; a duty to warn the employee of dangerous conditions; a duty to see that a sufficient number of suitable and competent fellow employees were provided to assist with the work; and a duty to promulgate and enforce rules to make the work safe.

Thus, the ability of an injured employee to recover compensation from his employer was limited to the case where the employee could prove that the employer had failed in one of these duties. The possibility of monetary recovery by an injured employee was further restricted by the common law defenses of "contributory negligence" and "assumption of risk". If the workman did not exercise reasonable care for his own safety, his recovery was barred by his own contributory negligence even though it involved only a momentary lapse of caution. The "fellow servant" rule was also available as a defense to the employer; the employee was deemed to have assumed the risk of being injured by a fellow employee.

As a natural consequence under the common law system the greater proportion of industrial accidents were uncompensated with the financial burden falling upon the person least able to bear it--the injured employee. In addition, litigation meant delay in collecting benefits and the injured employee was under pressure to compromise his claim for less than its true value in order to obtain necessities of life. These inequities led to the enactment of Workers' Compensation Insurance legislation in all states.

Workers' Compensation Insurance is based on the theory that the accident losses of industry are to be treated as a cost of production. Instead of being borne by the injured employee, the financial burden is shifted to the employer who is expected to add it to his costs in the form of insurance premiums, thus transferring the costs to consumers who purchase his product or service. Compulsory liability insurance helps to equalize the burden over an entire industry. The employer is charged with injuries arising out of his business without regard to any question of negligence either by himself or the employee. This is a compromise. The worker receives limited compensation, usually less than a jury in a court of law would award for his injuries, in exchange for an assurance that he will be expeditiously paid some amount in all events if the injury arises out of or during the course of his employment.

STATE LAWS APPLY

With the exception of coverage for certain groups such as longshoremen, harbor workers and

government employees, Workers' Compensation is
based on state law. Since each state has its own
statute, there is substantial variation in the
language of these statutes and benefits provided.
Most cover "all private employments". Some are
limited to "employments of a hazardous nature".
In a given case the law of more than one state may
be applicable giving the injured employee an
opportunity to choose the one most beneficial.
This situation can arise if an employee is injured
while working in a state different from that where
his employer has its main place of business.

WHO IS AN EMPLOYEE?

A person injured or killed must meet the technical
requirements as an employee if recovery is to be
made under Workers' Compensation coverage. If,
instead, he is an independent contractor at the time
of the accident, this coverage does not apply.

Generally, if the pilot is hired to do a job in his own
way without being under supervision or control of
the one who hired him, being responsible only for
accomplishing the given task, he is a "free lance"
or independent contractor. This distinction is not
always easy to make.

> For example, in a Texas case of
> somewhat questionable result a pilot
> was held to have been an independent
> contractor while engaged in aerial crop
> spraying, but became an employee upon
> termination of flying and beginning to
> repair the aircraft.

SCOPE OF EMPLOYMENT

Another prerequisite to recovery for injury or
death of an employee is that the activity in which
he is engaged must be within the scope of his
employment. If he is operating an aircraft for his
personal pleasure instead of for his employer's
benefit, he is not covered. Likewise, in most
states he is not covered if he is engaged in

unauthorized flight maneuvers such as buzzing a fishing boat, aerobatic flying, or violation of a state law.

MONETARY AMOUNT OF RECOVERY QUESTIONABLE

Although an injured employee is entitled to recover for his injury, the exact monetary amount to which he is entitled is often in question. A commissioner appointed by the state acts as a judge. This procedure frequently results in a grossly inadequate award for serious injury or death. Awards under Workers' Compensation laws generally are much lower than those made by juries for similar cases in civil court. For example, if an airline aircraft crashes killing fare-paying passengers and crew members, heirs of the fare-paying passengers will likely be entitled to compensation much greater than that collectible by heirs of the crew members. This is because heirs of the fare-paying passengers can sue the airline in a court of law; heirs of the crew members cannot since Workers' Compensation is the exclusive remedy. It is to be noted, however, that heirs of crew members might have legal recourse against third parties such as the aircraft manufacturer or the U.S. Government.

FEDERAL AVIATION ADMINISTRATION

In 1967 the Federal Aviation Agency became the Federal Aviation Administration (FAA) within the Department of Transportation and the aviation safety functions of the Civil Aeronautics Board were transferred to the National Transportation Safety Board (NTSB), Department of Transportation.

Although neither the Federal Aviation Administration nor the National Transportation Safety Board is part of the judicial system, the rules and regulations of these agencies have the force of law in their application to pilots.

TYPES OF FAA ENFORCEMENT ACTION

Depending on the particular fact situation, actions by the FAA are as follows:

1. Administrative action by a flight standards field inspector in the nature of a warning letter or letter of correction;

2. Action by the legal department to revoke or suspend a pilot's certificate;

3. Action by the legal department assessing a civil penalty;

4. Action by the legal department in revoking a medical certificate;

5. Action by the the Federal Air Surgeon in refusing to issue a medical certificate;

6. Action by the certification department in refusing to issue a pilot certificate;

7. Action by the legal department in seizing an aircraft involved in FAR violation .

SEIZURE OF AIRCRAFT INVOLVED IN FAR VIOLATION

An aircraft involved in violation of a Federal Aviation Regulation may be impounded on order of the Administrator if (1) the violation is of a type giving rise to a civil penalty and the Administrator has reason to believe the registered owner cannot or will not pay the penalty, or (2) the violation is of a more serious nature and the actions of the registered owner indicate the probability of future serious violations based on inability or unwillingness to comply with the FARs.

The act of seizure may be performed by a state or federal law enforcement officer or by an FAA safety inspector if an appropriate order has been issued by the FAA Regional Director or Area Manager.

After the aircraft is seized, it is to be placed in the nearest available and adequate public storage facility in the judicial district in which it is seized. Written notice of this seizure is sent by certified mail to the registered owner and to each person shown by FAA records to have an interest in it, stating the time, date and place of seizure, the name and address of the custodian of the aircraft, the reasons for the seizure, including the violations believed or judicially determined to have been committed, and the amount that may be tendered as a compromise of a civil penalty or payment for a civil penalty assessed by a District Court. The amount will include the costs of seizure, storage and maintenance.

RELEASE OF SEIZED AIRCRAFT

The administrator will issue an order releasing the aircraft whenever one of the following occurs:

1. The registered owner pays an agreed upon civil penalty, the costs of seizure, storage and maintenance of the aircraft;

2. The United States Attorney notifies the FAA that he refuses to institute collection proceedings;

3. A bond in the appropriate amount is deposited to cover any civil penalty, costs of seizure, storage and maintenance.

CRIMINAL REPORTS REQUIRED BY FAA INSPECTORS

In addition to their normal duties, FAA inspectors are required to report suspected violation of certain criminal laws. When appropriate, reports are to be made to the Federal Bureau of Investigation, the Bureau of Customs, the Federal Bureau of Narcotics and the Immigration and Naturalization Service.

The following are required to be reported:

1. Knowingly and willfully forging certificates;

2. Knowingly using or attempting to use a fraudulent certificate;

3. Knowingly and willfully displaying or causing to be displayed on any aircraft any marks that are false or misleading as to nationality or registration;

4. Interference with air navigation;

5. Making a false statement to a department or agency of the government;

6. Use of aircraft for illegal purposes;

7. Crimes committed aboard aircraft such as interference with flight crew members, carrying concealed weapons aboard aircraft, committing or attempting to commit aircraft piracy, committing robbery, mayhem or murder.

FAA ENFORCEMENT AND CERTIFICATION PROCEDURES

Enforcement and certification procedures of the FAA are designed to protect and enhance two interests: (1) the public interest in aviation safety; and (2) the individual interest of a pilot or other person charged with violation of Federal Aviation Regulations. In its role as overseer of the public interest the FAA must observe certain procedural steps intended to assure fair and efficient processing of a charge against an individual pilot, aircraft owner or business operator.

NATURE OF PROCEEDINGS

Although technically the FAA and the NTSB are administrative agencies rather than part of the

judicial system, certain of their procedures are
similar to those involved in a court of law and are
employed by FAA attorneys in proceedings before
administrative law judges. Knowledge by the
accused of certain basic procedures and their
implications is essential to avoid unnecessary
exposure to adverse consequences. Law judges of
the NTSB must conduct hearings in accordance with
officials rules established for this purpose.

Responsible and conscientious pilots, aircraft
owners and business operators are willing to
cooperate reasonably with the FAA and the NTSB in
maintaining a high level of aviation safety. There
is no legal or moral obligation, however, for them to
expose themselves to unreasonable adverse
consequences which might arise from misunderstanding, incomplete or inaccurate information.
The FAA has the burden of proof whenever a
violation is charged; the accused is under no legal
or moral obligation to do the FAA's work for it.

REPRESENTATION BY ATTORNEY

Should a pilot or aircraft owner faced with a
violation charge retain an attorney familiar with
enforcement procedures to represent him? There
is no legal requirement that a person be represented
by an attorney. The actual case reports published
by the NTSB show, however, that a pilot
representing himself will likely lose. The
proceeding is adversarial in nature and the FAA's
prosecuting attorney is a specialist in that type of
proceeding.

Although there are no guarantees that
representation by an attorney will result in a
"win", the accused will be given an opportunity for
a fair hearing and will not lose on procedural
grounds. It is imperative that the accused
effectively present his side of the controversy in a
manner procedurally acceptable to the law judge.
Merely telling of his "side of the story" to the law
judge will not usually vindicate the accused.

Certain ways in which an attorney may be of assistance include:

1. Persuading the FAA inspector to drop the charge;

2. Persuading the FAA inspector to dispose of the matter informally instead of bringing a formal charge;

3. Persuading the FAA attorneys to drop the charge;

4. Persuading the FAA attorneys to reduce the amount of a civil penalty

5. Persuading the FAA attorneys to reduce the period of suspension of the pilot's certificate;

6. Persuading the FAA attorneys not to revoke the pilot's certificate;

7. Communicating for the pilot so as to preclude later use of pilot's statements against him;

8. Preparation of the necessary formal documents;

9. Representation in formal proceedings before a hearing officer of the National Transportation Safety Board;

10. Representation in the United States District Court if the FAA attorney has referred collection of a civil penalty to the U. S. Attorney;

11. Representation in court proceedings if the pilot is not satisfied with the ruling of the National Transportation Safety Board.

In addition, the pilot might desire to engage the services of an attorney if the incident in question should lead to a civil suit against him, or it is of interest to the Federal Bureau of Investigation, the Bureau of Customs, the Federal Bureau of Narcotics, the Immigration and Naturalization

Service or local law enforcement agencies.

Although aviation qualified attorneys are not numerous, one may be found by calling the local city or county bar association referral service, or one of the larger aviation associations.

STATEMENTS BY PILOT

STATEMENT TO FAA INSPECTOR FOLLOWING ACCIDENT – CAUTION !

After having been involved in an accident or incident, a pilot may be requested by an FAA inspector to make a statement orally or in writing as to the cause and the surrounding circumstances. It is highly recommended the pilot defer making any such statement until he has had an opportunity to reflect on the incident and recover from any physical or emotional effect which might affect his clarity of thought. Although under these circumstances, the pilot might feel inclined to make a statement as a gesture of cooperation, rarely would there be any great benefit to anyone in doing so immediately. He is within his rights to refuse to make any statement and to seek the assistance of an attorney if he elects to do so. See CAUTION in PILOT'S REPLY under PROCEDURAL STEPS IN PROCESSING ALLEGED VIOLATIONS.

STATEMENT TO FBI, NTSB OR OTHER AUTHORITY

Aircraft accidents and incidents often result in investigation by the Federal Bureau of Investigation or other law enforcement authority. There is no legal compulsion on the pilot or other crew members to give a statement to these agencies. It is recommended no statement be made until there has been an opportunity to review details of the matter and confer with a legal representative since self-incrimination might otherwise be the result.

STATEMENT TO PILOT'S EMPLOYER

Although following an accident or incident the employer-employee relationship requires the pilot make a statement within a reasonable time upon request by his employer, this is not required immediately. Adequate delay for reflection and consultation is permissible. Moreover, this statement cannot be compelled in the presence of FAA, FBI or other government agents.

The pilot should use good judgment in reporting essential facts only. Notwithstanding his employer's good faith, the pilot's written statements may end up in files of the FAA or the courts and later be used against him.

PROCEDURAL STEPS IN PROCESSING ALLEGED VIOLATIONS

INFORMING WITNESSES

The first communication giving rise to a charge of Federal Aviation Regulations violation is usually in the form of a telephone call to the local FAA office. An inspector of the Flight Standards Department, using information furnished by the caller, will initiate investigation of the incident. The caller might be one of any number of interested persons, such as a police officer, a relative of the pilot who is concerned about his welfare, an FAA tower operator, a lifeguard who has just witnessed a low flight at the local beach, or an unfriendly business competitor. In addition, an inspector in the process of investigating an aircraft accident may acquire information leading him to believe a violation has occurred; this may come from discussion with the pilot or crew members, eye witnesses or other persons.

PRELIMINARY ACTION BY FLIGHT STANDARDS FIELD INSPECTOR

The inspector first makes an investigation of the evidence to determine if a violation has occurred.

His first contact with the pilot will be a personal call or a letter outlining the information in the inspector's possession. He will invite a reply indicating that statements by the pilot will be considered in reaching a decision as to whether or not a violation will be officially charged.

PILOT'S REPLY: CAUTION!

A word of **CAUTION** is in order at this point: Without his knowing it, the pilot is in an adversarial position opposite the FAA inspector as potential prosecutor! Since an accident or incident may lead to criminal or civil charges as well as charges of FAR violation, the pilot should give due deliberation before making any statements, oral or written; they may be later used against him. If he is represented by an attorney, the attorney's oral statements would not be used for adverse purposes in later proceedings. Further, the pilot is under no immediate duty to reply or make any statement whatsoever respecting the incident upon which the investigation is based. It may be to his advantage, at a later appropriate time, to provide the inspector any favorable or mitigating facts by submitting a formal report, if requested by the FAA. The pilot's verbal statements to the inspector--even by telephone--will be recorded in the inspector's personal notes. These notes may later be used for evidence purposes to "refresh" the inspector's memory if he is called to testify before a law judge as to what he was told by the pilot.

RECORD ACTIONS BY FLIGHT STANDARDS FIELD INSPECTOR

After completing his investigation, the inspector may determine the violation is not one that "affects safety", in which case he is authorized to dispose of the matter as "administrative action". This will normally consist of one of the following: (1) issuance of a warning letter, or (2) issuance of a letter of correction outlining an agreement between the inspector and the alleged violator that appropriate corrective action acceptable to the

FAA has been taken or will be taken within a specified time.

Although no penalty is assessed, the alleged violator's record maintained by the FAA will be scrutinized and taken into consideration in the event of later violations.

LEGAL ENFORCEMENT ACTION

If the Flight Standards Inspector determines a violation affecting safety has occurred, he will refer the matter to the office of the FAA Regional Counsel, recommending either certificate action or civil money penalty action. The referral letter will recite relative factors including mitigating or aggravating circumstances; status and background of the alleged violator; the pilot's compliance disposition, if known; position in aviation, including salary, if known; and any other information which can be used to reach a decision as to appropriate sanction. At this procedural point the FAA attorney may feel, after reviewing the file, that the burden of proving a violation cannot be met and close the file without any action being taken. Otherwise, he may commence an action seeking suspension or revocation of the pilot's certificate or assessing a civil penalty. He would normally not pursue both unless the violation was of a particularly grievous nature.

NOTICE OF PROPOSED CERTIFICATE ACTION

Except for an emergency order, prior to issuing an order affecting the pilot's certificate, the FAA legal department will issue a Notice of Proposed Certificate Action outlining the charges and facts upon which the action is proposed. The proposed action is usually stated as certificate suspension for a specified period.

PILOT'S RESPONSE TO NOTICE

In response to the Notice of Proposed Certificate Action, the pilot involved has the following choices:

1. He may admit the charges and surrender his certificate;

2. He may request that the FAA order be issued so as to expedite appeal to the National Transportation Safety Board;

3. He may answer the charges in writing (**CAUTION**);

4. He may request an informal conference with an FAA attorney;

5. He may take no action, in which case the Administrator will issue the proposed order.

If no response is made by the pilot he will be entitled to a formal hearing before a law judge after the FAA issues an order suspending the pilot's certificate.

WRITTEN ANSWER BY PILOT (SEE STATEMENTS BY PILOT)

If the pilot elects to answer the charges in writing, he should do so within the time period specified in the notice letter. **CAUTION.** There are important considerations to be given this answer: It becomes part of the pilot's record; any statements made therein may be later used to the pilot's disadvantage in an enforcement action to suspend or revoke his pilot certificate.

INFORMAL CONFERENCE WITH FAA ATTORNEY (CERTIFICATE ACTION)

If the pilot has requested an informal conference with an FAA attorney he may be able to present his side of the case and negotiate for a lesser penalty, such as having a threatened revocation reduced to suspension, reduction of the proposed period of suspension, or for the reduction of the amount of a proposed civil penalty. The outcome of this conference will depend on the relative strengths and weaknesses of the case, along with the FAA attorney's view as to seriousness of the charges. The FAA attorney has considerable discretionary authority at this stage.

It is important to keep in mind during this informal conference the FAA attorney's action will be based in part on his assessment of the pilot's future compliance with Federal Aviation Regulations. Thus, the pilot's attitude and disposition should be professional, sincere and businesslike; this is no time for belligerence, emotionalism or name-calling. **CAUTION.** There is an inherent danger that the FAA attorney will gain information from the pilot during this conference which will strengthen his resolve to prosecute the pilot. If the matter cannot be resolved through negotiations, the FAA attorney will issue an order, from which the pilot can appeal to the National Transportation Safety Board.

APPEAL TO NATIONAL TRANSPORTATION SAFETY BOARD

If the FAA Regional Counsel has issued an order revoking or suspending the pilot's certificate the pilot can request a hearing before an administrative law judge of the National Transportation Safety Board. This hearing is very much like a court proceeding. Prior to the hearing the law judge has the authority to subpoena witnesses and order documents produced. This includes authority to order the pilot to testify only if subpoenaed by the FAA.

Under former law a pilot who made statements only under the compulsion of a subpoena enjoyed certain immunities; the statements made could not be used against him in any future proceedings (except a perjury case). In October 1970, however, the President signed into law the "Organized Crime Control Act of 1970" (Public Law 90-452). This law repealed many of the existing laws which granted immunity and substituted a new rule. That part of the Federal Aviation Act, Section 1004(i), which formerly prevented a pilot's statements from being used against him when he testified under compulsion of a subpoena was one of the laws repealed. The new rule enacted in the October 1970 law is much more restrictive and protects pilots only against the use of their prior statements in subsequent "criminal" cases only. Therefore, the FAA now has the power to use pilot statements given under subpoena against the pilot in future certificate actions and probably in civil penalty cases as well.

Following a complete hearing the law judge may issue an order affirming the FAA order suspending or revoking the pilot's certificate, or dismiss the action for lack of adequate supporting evidence. The law judge may order the proceeding terminated upon payment by the pilot of a money penalty if the FAA is willing to accept a civil penalty instead of certificate action, and the pilot is willing to make payment. The judge does not, however, have authority to order payment of a civil penalty; this is a voluntary undertaking between the pilot and the FAA attorney. In reality, a civil penalty compromise settlement cannot often be effected at this late stage in the proceedings. A third course of action available to the law judge is reduction of the proposed period of suspension while affirming the FAA's charges of FAR violation.

If the accused pilot is not content to let stand an order of the law judge relating to his certificate, he can pursue the matter further in the following sequence:

1. Appeal to the full five-member National Transportation Safety Board,

2. Further appeal to the U. S. Circuit Court of Appeals;

3. Finally, petition for a discretionary review by the United States Supreme Court.

CIVIL PENALTY (FINE)

Upon referral from the Flight Standards Inspector,

the Regional Counsel may determine the violation
charges to be of a relatively non-serious nature,
such as those involving failure to accomplish
inspections, lack of documentation, flight time
limitations, etc. Thus, the attorney in charge may
seek a money penalty rather than certificate
revocation or suspension. A money penalty of up
to $1,000 may be assessed for each violation. This
is the maximum amount authorized by the Federal
Aviation Act for each violation. As a practical
matter penalties assessed against pilots for single
violations are usually considerably lower than
$1,000.00. Assessments against business operators
may amount to many times that amount if there have
been repetitive violations, e.g., $1000.00 for each
flight of an unairworthy aircraft.

NOTICE OF CIVIL PENALTY

If the FAA Legal Department determines a civil
money penalty is in order, a letter will be mailed to
the alleged violator outlining the alleged violation
and stating an amount acceptable to settle the
matter by compromise. The amount will be
determined after considering all surrounding and
mitigating circumstances and may be reduced if the
pilot can present a satisfactory reason.

INFORMAL CONFERENCE (CIVIL PENALTY)

Although in civil penalty matters the FAA is not
legally obligated to provide the opportunity for an
informal conference, as a matter of policy such
conferences are encouraged by the FAA. This is
an opportunity for the accused pilot to inform the
FAA attorney of additional facts warranting a
reduction in the amount of the penalty, or a
dropping the charges. The same CAUTION applies as
that stated in relation to INFORMAL CONFERENCE
concerning certificate suspension or revocation.
The attorney may gain information from the pilot
which will strengthen his resolve to proceed against
the pilot.

REISSUANCE OF CERTIFICATE AFTER SUSPEN-
SION OR REVOCATION

At the end of a specified period of suspension the pilot can resume his privileges as they previously existed. Where a license revocation has been effected, however, he must qualify all over again, complying with whatever testing or checking is required by the FAA. An application for a new license will normally not be accepted for one year following revocation.

MEDICAL CERTIFICATE DENIAL OR REVOCATION

A pilot may lose the value of his pilot's certificate if the Federal Air Surgeon or a local aviation medical examiner refuses to issue an appropriate medical certificate, or if the FAA Administrator using his emergency authority revokes the pilot's medical certificate. In each instance, however, the medical problem must be such that it would "probably interfere with the safe piloting of aircraft"; the mere possibility of such interference is not a sufficient basis for denial.

Procedures for pursuing the pilot's rights are different in denial and revocation cases and are outlined below.

EMERGENCY REVOCATION BY FAA ADMINIS-TRATOR

Whenever the Administrator has strong reason to believe a pilot is not physically fit to exercise the privileges of his medical certificate, the Administrator has a duty as overseer of the public interest to ground the pilot by withdrawing the medical certificate.

If the Administrator revokes the pilot's medical certificate and the pilot appeals to the National Transportation Safety Board, the Administrator has the burden of justifying his revocation action. The pilot is entitled to an expedited hearing before an administrative law judge. The Administrator must prove by a preponderance of reliable medical evidence that the pilot is not qualified to hold a medical certificate.

At this hearing the pilot is entitled to have his own medical experts testify, and to testify in his own behalf, in support of his qualification to hold a medical certificate.

AVIATION MEDICAL EXAMINER'S REFUSAL TO CERTIFY

Upon refusal by an FAA designated physician or the Federal Air Surgeon to issue a medical certificate, the pilot must initiate appeal proceedings if he desires to question the validity of the decision.

Two FAA discretionary avenues are open immediately: (1) The pilot can petition the Federal Air Surgeon for reconsideration of the denial; (2) petition the FAA Administrator for special issuance. With both procedures the medical evidence of the pilot's condition will be evaluated by medical experts before the petition is either granted or denied.

APPEAL TO NATIONAL TRANSPORTATION BOARD

If the Federal Air Surgeon refuses to issue a medical certificate, the pilot can then proceed to file with the National Transportation Safety Board a petition for review of the Administrator's action. A law judge will weigh the medical evidence presented by the pilot as well as that presented by the Administrator before deciding if a medical certificate should be issued or denied.

A very important feature of this proceeding is that the pilot has the burden of proof respecting his medical qualification. This differs from the procedure in which the Administator has exercised his emergency authority in revoking the pilot's medical certificate. The pilot will be required to present documentation and testimony of medical experts to prove that his condition meets FAR medical standards.

FURTHER REVIEW

If the pilot is unsuccessful in the hearing before

the NTSB law judge, he can petition the full five-member Board for a review. The board has the authority to overrule or sustain the law judge's decision. Further review is permitted in the U. S. Circuit Court of Appeals; beyond that a request may be made for discretionary review by the U. S. Supreme Court.

LIENS, ENCUMBRANCES AND SECURITY INTERESTS

Since lien laws vary widely with different states, the applicable state law should be reviewed in any particular situation if the question of lien rights and security interests arises. A lien or encumbrance against an aircraft is a charge imposed on a specific aircraft by which it becomes security for performance of a certain obligation. A lien is not a property interest, but only a security right in the aircraft lasting until the obligation is performed. A lien or encumbrance may be voluntary or involuntary, possessory or nonpossessory. Liens and encumbrances most commonly associated with aircraft are:

1. Mechanics' liens,

2. Chattel mortgages,

3. Conditional sales agreements,

4. FAA imposed liens,

5. Federal law imposed liens.

MECHANICS' LIENS

An involuntary possessory lien may arise if maintenance or repair work is performed and the person doing the work desires to hold the aircraft as security until paid. This right may be lost, however, if possession of the aircraft is relinquished prior to payment. The law cannot be said to be entirely settled as to mechanics' lien rights if there is an existing recorded mortgage or conditional sale contract. Generally speaking, if the claimant had actual or constructive notice of the previously recorded documents, he would not be given priority.

CHATTEL MORTGAGE

A chattel mortgage is a nonpossessory encumbrance voluntarily created by an aircraft owner. It arises by agreement and it is frequently given as security in return for a purchase-money loan made by a bank or other financing institution. A chattel mortgage should be recorded with the FAA Aircraft Registry Office. After the aircraft owner has satisfied the obligation, a release signed by the lender should also be filed with the FAA so as to clear the owner's title.

CONDITIONAL SALE

A conditional sale arises by agreement between the seller and the purchaser. The purchaser takes possession and exercises all rights incident to ownership of the aircraft. Title does not pass to the buyer, however, until a particular condition is satisfied. The most common condition is full payment of the purchase price. The buyer is subject to laws and regulations applicable to aircraft owners even though he has not received title. The seller retains a security interest which should be evidenced by a written agreement, the original of which should be recorded with the FAA Aircraft Registry Office.

FEDERAL AVIATION ACT

An involuntary possessory lien may arise under the Federal Aviation Act. Under this Act an aircraft involved in violation of certain FARs is subject to a lien as security for payment by the owner of any civil penalty later assessed against him and may be summarily seized following a violation.

FEDERAL LAW

An involuntary possessory lien may arise under Federal law. An aircraft may be seized by a designated authority and subjected to a lien for activities violating Customs, Public Health and Postal laws and regulations.

SALE OF AIRCRAFT TO SATISFY LIEN

In certain states a lien holder may sell the aircraft to satisfy a debt that has not been paid. The proper state procedure must be followed, which typically requires prior adequate notice be given the aircraft owner by certified mail. In certain states a court judgment must be rendered against the owner before an aircraft can be sold to satisfy a lien.

RECORDING: STATE/COUNTY

Certain states and counties have statutes relating to creation and recording of liens relating to aircraft. These control such matters as financing statements and liens for labor, storage and materials. If a lien is created it should be recorded with the Federal Aviation Administration.

RECORDING WITH FAA

The FAA recording system merely establishes priorities if there are conflicting claims. It does not create lien rights. If there are conflicting claims the claimant first to record its interest will be given priority.

Documents which are to be recorded with the FAA should be mailed to:

Aircraft Registry Office
P. O. Box 25504
Oklahoma City, Oklahoma 73125

ILLUSTRATIVE COURT CASES

ABSENCE OF ENGINE OIL IN LEASED AIRCRAFT, LESSOR'S LIABILITY

In an unusual decision by the New Mexico Supreme Court, in the case of **Rudisaile v. Hawk Aviation, Inc.**, the aircraft lessor was held liable for death of a renter-pilot who, in failing to conduct a preflight inspection, did not discover absence of engine oil.

The aircraft had been released following partial service during which the oil had been drained and a new filter installed, but new oil had not been added. The engine failed shortly following takeoff with a crash resulting. The court held that under New Mexico law the aircraft was in a "defective condition" when it was delivered to the renter-pilot, thus, the lessor was liable.

EDITORIAL COMMENT: This case demonstrates that the theory of "strict liability" has been extended to lessors of defective aircraft as well as to manufacturers.

AERONAUTICAL CHART ERROR, NONLIABILITY OF U. S. GOVERNMENT

The United States District Court, District of Kansas, in the case of **Baird v. United States of America**, held that the U. S. Government was not liable for an error in a Sectional Aeronautical Chart relating to airport lighting. The pilot of a Piper Seneca which crashed contended the U. S. Government should be held liable for publishing information indicating a lighted runway 2800 feet in length, when in fact only 2176 feet of a shorter runway was lighted.

The court held that publication of the information by the U. S. Government, through the

Federal Aviation Administration was a "discretionary function" as opposed to a "mandatory" function, thus, the doctrine of sovereign immunity prevented recovery against the United States.

COUNTY AIRPORTS, BIRD-CAUSED CRASH, IMMUNITY

The United States Court of Appeals, Fifth Circuit, in the case of **Miree et al**, held that under Georgia law DeCalb County was immune from suit based on a bird-caused crash. The plaintiff had contended he was a third-party beneficiary of a contract between DeCalb County and the Federal Aviation Administration created by a Federal grant agreement. The court found against the plaintiff in rejecting this theory, as well as declaring the county's sovereign immunity from suit under theories of negligence or nuisance.

SALES TAX - LEASED AIRCRAFT - ENGINE PARTS

The California Court of Appeal, Second District, enunciated the distinction for taxation purposes between sale of parts used to modify engines on aircraft used in common carriage and sale of such aircraft as a whole.

In **National Aircraft Leasing, Ltd., v. State Board of Equalization**, the court held the State could levy a sales or use tax in the amount of $12,446.54 for parts and labor associated with modification of engines on a Lockheed Hercules. This was so, even though no sales tax would have been applicable upon sale of the aircraft since it was in use exclusively for common carriage, and a California statute exempted such aircraft from sales tax.

AIRCRAFT STALL ACCIDENT - SLIDING PILOT'S SEAT

In a Wisconsin case, **Goodwin et al, v. Cessna Aircraft,** the Court of Appeals found that a Cessna 172-M was in a defective condition when it stalled shortly after takeoff. The pilot, who was only 5 feet 6 inches tall, had positioned his seat all the way forward, thinking it was locked in place. As the aircraft started to climb, the seat slipped backward causing the pilot to pull back on the control yoke. Three passengers were injured in the ensuing crash. The jury found Cessna 35% at fault and the pilot 65% at fault.

EDITORIAL COMMENT: This case demonstrates application of two theories concerning legal liability: (1) strict liability of the manufacturer for results of an aircraft design defect, and (2) shifting of fault partially to a pilot who fails to exercise reasonable care for his own safety.

THUNDERSTORM TURBULENCE, PILOT'S RESPONSI-BILITY, AIR TRAFFIC CONTROL

In the case of **Associated Aviation Underwriters, et al, v. United States of America,** decided by the United States District Court, Northern District of Texas, the crash of a Piper Aztec E was found to be the fault of the pilot. The aircraft apparently encountered severe turbulence when flying parallel to and approximately 10 miles from a line of thunderstorms whose tops reached to 60,000 feet. In addition to information provided by his airborne radar, the pilot was advised by air traffic controllers of the location of the thunderstorms.

The court found the pilot solely responsible for the crash on the basis that he was primarily responsible for the safe operation of the aircraft. He should have stayed alert in the course of his flight, and, since the weather conditions were clearly unfavorable, he was obligated to look for and avoid the hazardous conditions.

CIVIL PENALTY ACTION BY FAA AGAINST PERSON ENGAGED IN BROKERAGE ACTIVITIES

A rather unusual action was taken by the FAA in the case of **Marshall Landy v. The Federal Aviation Administration, et al,** United States District Court, Southern District of New York.

After seizure of a Boeing 707 allegedly having been operated in violation of certain Federal Aviation Regulations , the FAA instituted civil penalty action against the lessee of the aircraft and a person engaged in certain brokerage-type activities. These included locating shippers, forwarding sublessees to shippers, arranging to provide flight crews, prearranging points of departure and preparing documents and collecting funds.

The court found that these activities brought the broker within the definition of "aircraft operator", since he had caused or authorized the operation of the aircraft as that term is used in the Federal Aviation Act.

EDITORIAL COMMENT: Enforcement action which can be taken by the FAA includes suspension or revocation of any FAA-issued certificates held by the violator, or in the alternative, imposition of a civil penalty. If the violator holds no certificate, the FAA is limited to civil penalty action. This can be up to a maximum of $1000.00 for each violation.

NEGLIGENCE OF AIR TRAFFIC CONTROLLER – LIABILITY OF U. S. GOVERNMENT, AIRCRAFT CRASH

In the case of **Joyce H. Martin, et al, v. United States of America, et al,** decided by the United States Court of Appeals, Eighth Circuit, the court found the U. S. Government liable for the crash of a twin-engine Cessna after receipt by the pilot from air traffic controllers of erroneous weather information.

Following a missed approach at Grider Field near Pine Bluff, Arkansas, the pilot requested and received clearance for a second approach. He also received a new altimeter setting which was incorrect and resulted in an indication that during the second approach the aircraft was 100 feet higher than its actual altitude. The pilot was not informed of deteriorating weather conditions with visibility reduced from one mile to three quarters of a mile, and of a ceiling reduction from 300 feet to zero.

The court reasoned that the pilot would not have attempted the second approach if he had received accurate weather information, thus the air traffic controllers were at fault and the U. S. Government was liable.

LIABILITY OF AIRCRAFT MANUFACTURER – NOSE GEAR DEFECT

The law of Louisiana as indicated by the decision of **Charlie Hirston Aircraft, Inc., et al, v. Beech Aircraft Corporation, et al,** decided by the U. S. District Court, Western District of Louisiana, appears to differ from that of the law of certain other states as it relates to a manufacturer's liability for an aircraft design defect.

Because of a defect in the nose gear of a 1971 Beech Duke A-60, a landing was made in which substantial damage was sustained by the aircraft, its engines and propellers. No persons were injured and no other property was damaged.

The court found the nose gear to have been defective at the time of leaving the factory and allowed recovery for the cost of repairs to the aircraft and other related incidental expenses. The court further indicated that recovery for loss of income or loss of profits while the aircraft was out of service would have been recoverable upon proper proof by the plaintiff.

EDITORIAL COMMENT: In most states a manufacturer's liability is limited to personal injury or death caused by a defectively designed or manufactured aircraft, or for damage caused to other property, but not for damage to the subject aircraft except to the extent of any current sales warranty.

CROP SPRAYING, LIABILITY FOR GARDEN DAMAGE

In the Louisiana Court of Appeals case of **Weldon Himel, et al, v. American Employers' Insurance Company, et al,** owners of certain gardens situated near a cane field brought a court action for destruction of their okra, beans, corn, peas, peppers, tomatoes and pumpkins caused by the chemical 2-4-D which had been released from a helicopter spraying operation. The owner of the cane field was held liable under a provision of the Louisiana law which stated: "Although a proprietor may do with his estate whatever he pleases, still he cannot make any work on it which may deprive his neighbor of the liberty of enjoying his own, or which may be the cause of any damage to him". Owners of the gardens were allowed to recover the reasonable value of their destroyed vegetables even though they were intended for home consumption rather than sale.

AIRCRAFT OWNERS'S LIABILITY FOR PILOT'S NEGLIGENCE

The District Court of the State of Idaho, in the case of **Rueben Weber, et al, v. Lee Emmett Moyle, et al,** held that negligence of the plot lessee was not imputed by law to the owner-lessor of the aircraft. The plaintiff had contended since the flight was interstate, the liability was imposed on the owner-lessor by virtue of the Federal Aviation Act. The court disagreed, however, finding that neither the Federal Aviation Act nor Idaho law imposed liability on the owner-lessor merely because of the relationship with the lessee.

EDITORIAL COMMENT: Certain states, e.g., California, do hold an owner liable for negligence of a pilot who is operating an aircraft with the owner's consent.

AIRCRAFT SALE "AS IS" AGREEMENT

The Texas Supreme Court in the case of **Midcontinent Aircraft Corporation v. Curry County Spraying Service, Inc., et al,** rendered an opinion as to the meaning of "as is" in an aircraft sales agreement.

A wrecked single engine spray plane had been rebuilt along with the overhaul of its engine. A later engine failure resulted in a forced landing with substantial damage to the fuselage and wings. The pilot was not injured, however, and no other property damage resulted.

The owner/purchaser commenced suit, based on strict liability of the previous owner/seller under Rules of Tort law, to recover for his economic loss. The court held, however, that since no injury, death or damage to other property resulted, the seller was not liable on a tort theory for damage to the aircraft itself. Further, the previous sale/purchase transaction contained an "as is" agreement negating any express or implied warranties as to contractual liability for the damage.

WAKE TURBULENCE ACCIDENT - ATC NEGLIGENCE

In the case of **Zoltan Szilard, et al, v. United**

States of America, et al, decided by the United States District Court, Central District of California, the U. S. Government was found liable for the crash of a Piper PA 28-140.

The Piper had been conducting touch-and-go landings at the Van Nuys Airport when it crashed following an encounter with turbulence created by the wake of a military C-130 which had departed from a parallel runway. The tower had issued a cautionary warning of possible turbulence "on your liftoff". Turbulence was encountered, however, while the Piper was approaching the runway some 200 feet from the threshold.

The court found the Government liable on the basis of failure of a tower controller to issue an accurate warning to the Piper pilot.

AIRCRAFT USE TAX - NAVIGABLE AIR SPACE

A rather unusual decision was rendered by the United States District Court, District of New Mexico in **Stahmann Farms, Inc., v. United States of America.**
Stahmann had utilized three aircraft, a Piper PA-18, a Lockheed PV-2 and a Boeing Stearman for agricultural activities over certain pecan orchards. The aircraft had been flown from and to the owner's landing facilities only. The owner argued it was not subject to the use tax imposed by the Federal Aviation Act, contending the aircraft had not been used in navigable air space as contemplated by the Act. The court upheld the IRS, however, holding the navigable air space included that needed to insure safety in takeoff and landing of aircraft associated with private facilities as well as public facilities. Thus, the owner was found liable for taxes.

PARACHUTE TRAINING SCHOOL - RESPONSIBILITY

RELEASE

The New York Supreme Court, Appellate Division, in the case of **Bruce E. Goss v. William Sweet, dba: Stormville Parachute Center, et al,** had occasion to interpret and construe a responsibility release executed by a student when enrolling in a parachute training school.

After receiving approximately one hour of on-land training, the student was taken to an altitude of 2800 feet. Pursuant to instruction, he jumped from the airplane, breaking his leg when landing. He had previously signed a "responsibility release" purporting to waive any and all claims against the training school and assuming full responsibility for any damage or injury caused while participating in the sport.

In reviewing New York law, the court stated that while agreements intended to absolve a party from liability for his own negligence are closely scrutinized and strictly construed, they will be enforced by the courts absent some special legal relationship between the parties, or some overriding public interest. There must be be a clear understanding between the parties which plainly and precisely defines the limitation of liability. In this case the training school allegedly violated a number of Federal Aviation Regulations during the undertaking leading to the student's injuries. This being the situation, the previously signed responsibility release was not binding against the student.

NEGLIGENT CROP SPRAYING

The Nebraska Supreme Court in the case of **Mustion v. Ealt,** affirmed a lower court judgment awarding damages for loss of cattle poisoned by a chemical compound which drifted from adjacent property. The chemical Thimet was found in the soil and alfalfa samples of both plaintiff's and defendant's property, as well as plaintiff's water supply. The court found that this contamination resulted in the death of six of plaintiff's cows.

EDITORIAL COMMENT: This decision is in keeping with the well-established rule of law that a person operating an airplane for spraying crops must use due care to perform such operations under such conditions and in such manner as not to cause injury or loss to other property owners. Chemicals may end up on adjacent property due to wind conditions or inadvertent release by a spray aircraft pilot.

UNSAFE AIRPORT

In a Kansas case, **Federal Insurance Company v. United States of America,** decided by the District Court of Kansas, the U. S. Government was found to be liable for the crash of a Beechcraft Model K-35.

The pilot had attempted to abort a landing at a grass strip situated on land owned by the U. S. and which was operated and maintained by the Corps of Engineers. The strip was open for use by the public but was unattended. Vegetation on the landing strip was over knee-high in some places. Also the surface soil of the landing strip was soft and muddy in some areas due to earlier heavy rains. The pilot apparently discovered the true condition upon touchdown and attempted to take off without stopping. After contacting a fence, the aircraft crashed.

Under Kansas law, the operator of an airport open to the public is under a duty to maintain it in a safe condition and to warn potential users of any unsafe conditions. The court found the Corps of Engineers and the FAA had been negligent in failing to control the height of the grass and failing to mark the airfield as unsafe so as to warn pilots contemplating its use. Significantly, the court further found the pilot not contributorily negligent. He had found himself in an emergency situation not of his own making and could not be faulted for attempting to take off without stopping.

AIRCRAFT USE TAX

In the case of **Pope & Talbot, Inc., v. The Department of Revenue,** decided by the Washington State Supreme Court, the State of Washington was required to refund some $4000 collected for use of aircraft within the state.

The subject aircraft was owned by an Oregon corporation and used to transport its executives and customers between Portland and certain points within Washington. The court found imposition of a Washington tax improper on two bases: 1) although the aircraft was an article of tangible personal property as contemplated by the Washington Tax Statute, its transportation into the state had not "finally ended" as required by the statute; (2) imposition of such a tax violated the commerce clause of the U. S. Constitution.

RECORDATION OF AIRCRAFT INTERESTS

The Florida First District Court of Appeals in the case of **O'Neill v. Barnett Bank of Jacksonville, N.A.,** pointed out a subtle but important principle regarding priority of conflicting interests. A fixed base operator had purchased an aircraft to be used for rental purposes, executing a financing security agreement. Although the aircraft was not part of a sales inventory, the FBO sold the aircraft to a third party who did not make a title search prior to the time of purchase.

The court found that under Florida law the buyer had not purchased the aircraft in the ordinary course of business, since the FBO's business was not primarily sales of aircraft. Thus, the previously recorded finance security interest was superior.

COMMENT: This case and others referenced in this publication point to areas of considerable confusion and misunderstanding regarding recording of aircraft interests with the FAA Aircraft Registry Office situated at Oklahoma City.

Certain principles should be kept in mind: (1 Recording with the FAA does not create a title to the subject aircraft, but merely establishes notice of the recorder's priority; (2) For a title to be valid it must first be created in accordance with the law of the state in which the transfer is consummated. The various states have different laws governing transfer of interest in aircraft which must be satisfied before recording with the FAA can be of any value; (3) The U. S. Supreme Court in a 1983 case held that for an interest in an aircraft to be recognized, it must be recorded with the FAA Aircraft Registry Office. Time of recording will determine the priority to be given any claim.

AIRCRAFT SALE – MECHANIC'S LIEN – RECORDED LIEN

In a Florida District Court of Appeal case, **Commerce and Finance Company v. The Indiana National Bank,** the court resolved a conflict between a mechanic's lien for labor and parts and a previously recorded installment sales contract. A financing company had financed the purchase of a Cessna 401 and duly registered its interest with the FAA Registry Office. Thereafter, a corporation providing mechanical services and storage space sold the aircraft pursuant to a Florida statute for $900 due for services.

The new owner contended he took title free and clear of all previous encumbrances. The court disagreed, however, holding the aircraft to be subject to the interest of the financing company which had duly recorded its security interest in the aircraft.

RECORDING OF AIRCRAFT INTERESTS – PROPERTY

In the case of **Sanders v. M. D. Aircraft Sales Inc. and General Electric Credit Corporation,** decided by the U. S. Court of Appeals, Third Circuit, a question of priority of conflicting interests was resolved.

An aircraft dealer had financed a Piper Arrow, executing an agreement wherein the aircraft was pledged as security. The finance company recorded this agreement with the FAA Aircraft Registry in Oklahoma City. The agreement gave the dealer express power to sell the aircraft in the normal course of business. The aircraft was in fact sold but the seller failed to remit payment to the finance company. The court held that the purchaser had priority of interest even though the finance company had previously recorded its security ageemen. Looking to Pennsylvania law which determines validity of the two transactions, the court found that the buyer had aquire good title notwithstanding the financing company's previously recorded security interest.

COMMENT: Under a 1983 U. S. Supreme Court decision, the lienholder first to record its interest will have priority irrespective of any conflicting state law.

RECORDATION OF AIRCRAFT INTEREST

CIM International v. United States of America, U. S. District Court, Central District of California, a Nevada corporation purchased a 1953 Beechcraft, giving as consideration, in part, a purchase money security agreement in the

amount of $37,092.34. The seller did not record
this security agreement with the FAA Aircraft
Registry. Some ten months later both the seller
and the buyer transferred their respective
interests by bill of sale to a third party. In
the interim, however, the U. S. had filed notices
of federal tax liens against the original buyer,
thereafter seizing the aircraft from the
possession of the new buyer.

The court held that the tax lien took priority
over the buyer's interest since the original
seller failed to record its security agreement
and the U. S. Government had properly filed its
notices of tax liens with the Secretary of the
State of Nevada.

UNMARKED TV TOWER GUY WIRES

In the Michigan case of **Reminga, e al, v. United
States of America,** decided by the U. S. Court of
Appeals, the court decided the U. S.
Government's responsibility for the death of
three passengers in an aircraft that struck
unmarked guy wires. The FAA had approved
construction of a 1720 foot tower, properly
marked, but later issued an aeronautical
sectional chart depicting the wrong location of
the tower. The Government argued that approval
of the tower installation was a "discretionary
function" for which the Government was immune
from liability. The court agreed with this
argument regarding installation. It found,
however, that publication and distribution of
the sectional chart wrongly marked was a
"ministerial" function for which the Government
was found liable.

**PILOT   LICENSE   SUSPENSION,   OPERATION   OF
UNAIRWORTHY AIRCRAFT**

In a California case the U. S. Court of Appeals
upheld the FAA's action in suspending a pilot's
certificate for violation of FAR Sections 91.9
and 91.29(a). The engine of an aircraft which

the pilot was attempting to start caught fire. In the course of previous maintenance the generator had been disconnected and the electrical wiring left hanging loose. This led to the fire. The pilot argued that merely starting the engine did not constitute "operation" as the word was used in FARs. The court disagreed on the basis that starting the engine was for the purpose of air navigation and that the aircraft was not at the time in airworthy condition.

COLLISON WITH RADIO TOWER, U.S. GOVERNMENT LIABLE

In the case of **Fos, e al, v. United States of America,** decided by the U. S. Court of Appeals, the FAA was found to be at fault for the collision of a light aircraft with a radio tower. The FAA had previously established a traffic pattern altitude of 800 feet above mean sea level for the Fullerton Airport. A radio tower 819 feet high existed less than 2 miles away. FAA employees had been earlier cautioned regarding this situation, but had published no warnings concerning the hazard. While flying in the traffic pattern, the deceased pilot was apparently unable to see the tower due to rays of the sinking sun and visibility reduced by haze. Thus, the FAA was held to be at fault.

COLLISION WITH RADIO TOWER, U. S. GOVERNMENT NOT LIABLE

In a Michigan case of **Knight, e al, v. United States of America,** the court found the Government not liable for the crash of an aircraft which contacted several guy wires of a radio transmitting tower at an altitude of 360 feet above ground level. The tower was appropriately marked and was some 500 feet high. The pilot was conducting a cross-country flight in conditions of visibility less than one mile at the time of collision. The pilot's conduct was found to be the sole legal cause of the accident.

These reports are digests of appeals cases in which the Federal Aviation Administration has taken certificate action against the certificate holder, or has refused to issue a certificate. Following a hearing before a law judge the certificate holder can further appeal to the five-member National Transportation Safety Board.

Medical Certificate
PETITION OF WACZEWSKI, DOCKET SM-2965, FEBRUARY 1983.

A commercial pilot applied for a third-class airman medical certificate. He was denied a certificate on the basis of "history of cardiac arrhythmia as demonstrated by electrocardiographic (EKG) exercise stress testing, which condition requires medication for control". The pilot testified that he had taken Quinidine and Inderal for his irregular heartbeat. The pilot did not back up his testimony with that of a medical expert. The FAA presented an expert medical witness who testified that, in his opinion, the pilot was not qualified for a medical certificate. The law judge dismissed the pilot's petition on the basis that he had failed to prove his case.

EDITORIAL COMMENT: This case illustrates a procedural point not understood by many pilots seeking medical certification. If the FAA has refused to issue a medical certificate the pilot has the burden of proving that he is qualified for a medical certificate. The law judge must consider testimony of qualified medical experts regarding the pilot's qualification. No matter how credible the pilot may be in testifying on his own behalf, he is not a medical expert and his testimony is of little value.

Medical Certificate
PETITION OF STEFFEY, DOCKET SM-2966, FEBRUARY 1983.

A male, 70 years of age, applied for a third-class airman medical certificate, which was denied by the FAA. The petitioner had a history of mild hypertension for which he had been taking Hydrodiurill and Thiazide. The petitioner presented two medical experts who, in essence, testified that he was qualified for a pilot medical certifiate. The FAA presented its medical expert who testified that in his opinion the petitioner was not qualified for a medical certificate. After evaluating all evidence presented, the law judge ruled the petitioner had not sustained the burden of proving that he was qualified for a medical certificate, thus, sustaining the FAA's refusal.

Medical Certificate
PETITION OF HODGES, DOCKET SM-3024, FEBRUARY 1983.

A commercial pilot applied for a first-class airman medical certificate. The FAA denied the application on the basis that the petitioner had a medical history and diagnosis of anti-social personality disorder, which had been manifested by repeated overt acts. Evidence presented at the hearing revealed the petitioner had a history of 1) conviction for marijuana possession, 2) conspiracy to import a controlled substance, and 3) felon in possession of a firearm. In addition he had 8 convictions for speeding, with involvement in 4 motor vehicle accidents, the last of which resulted in suspension of his driver's license. The law judge agreed with the FAA that this was sufficient evidence of manifested overt acts to indicate a personality disorder severe enough to disqualify the pilot for a medical certificate.

Pilot
HELMS V. THOMPSON, DOCKET NO. SE-5643, FEBRUARY
1983.

The FAA issued an emergency order revoking the
pilot's commercial pilot certificate. He was
charged with having flown an experimental Breezy
aircraft over a heavily concentrated assembly of
persons at the Founder's Day celebration at
Zanesville, Ohio. Certain police officers
testified that the aircraft passed 40 to 50 feet
above river bridges on which numerous people
were gathered. The officers testified they
visually identified the pilot during these
flights. The pilot testified on his own behalf,
without the assistance of an attorney, and
stated that he was not the pilot of the aircraft
on any of the three passes that had been observed
by the FAA's witnesses. He did not present any
other witnesses to verify his testimony. The
law judge sustained the FAA's charges, but
reduced the sanction to a 10-month suspension
instead of revocation of the pilot's
certificate.

EDITORIAL COMMENT: This pilot did not take
advantage of an opportunity to present his own
witnesses to prove that the FAA's witnesses were
mistaken in identifying him as the pilot. The
mere fact that he owned the Breezy would not have
made him subject to a license suspension if some
other pilot was in fact flying it during the low
passes. Although a 10-month suspension is a
severe sanction, it is not as severe as
revocation. Following the specified period of
suspension, the pilot is free to resume all
piloting privileges, whereas, following a
revocation, the pilot must commence all over
again applying for a new pilot certificate. The
FAA can require that he pass written
examinations as well as flight tests, and will
not usually entertain an application for at

least 12 months following revocation.

Pilot
HELMS V. JOHNSON, DOCKET NO. SE 5665, FEBRUARY
1983.

A private pilot with 8000 flying hours and a violation-free history applied for an instrument rating. During the course of the written examination, he had in his possession written material that was also covered on the written examination. The FAA proposed to revoke his pilot certificate. The pilot requested a hearing before a law judge, representing himself, without the benefit of a lawyer. At the hearing he admitted the charges, offering only the excuse that he did not intend to refer to the unauthorized written material. The judge was not favorably impressed by this excuse. He affirmed the FAA's order revoking the pilot's certificate.

EDITORIAL COMMENT: Like many pilots, this one did not understand the significance of a hearing before a law judge. It is intended as an adversary proceeding in which the pilot can require the FAA to prove its charges. By openly admitting the charges, the pilot in this case left the law judge no alternative but to impose a sanction. The judge stated, "What we are concerned with here is the character and personal judgment being utilized by a person who flies an aircraft in this country." The judge in this respect agreed with the FAA that the pilot was not qualified to hold a pilot certificate.

Pilot
HELMS V. THOMPSON, DOCKET SE-5091, FEBRUARY 1983

The commercial pilot had been charged by the FAA with 7 FAR violations, with a proposed 60-day suspension of his pilot certificate. Just

prior to a scheduled hearing before a law judge,
the pilot and an FAA attorney agreed to a civil
penalty settlement instead of a license
suspension. The pilot agreed to pay a total of
$500 in exchange for the FAA's withdrawing the
charges. He failed to follow through, however,
after paying only $100.

The FAA reinstated the charges, proposing to
suspend the pilot's license for a period of 45
days, giving credit for the amount he had paid
toward his civil penalty. In a subsequent
hearing before a law judge, the pilot was unable
to give a satisfactory reason for not paying the
remaining $400 civil penalty. The judge
sustained the FAA's suspension of the pilot's
certificate for a period of 45 days.

EDITORIAL COMMENT: The facts of this case are
not stated in the report so as to explain why the
pilot would not take advantage of the civil
penalty payment rather than have his pilot's
license suspended. Payment of a civil penalty
is not an admission that any violation has taken
place and the pilot's record will not show that a
violation has occurred. If the civil penalty is
in a substantial amount, the FAA will usually
allow the pilot to pay it in installments. In
the eyes of most pilots, this is much more
desirable than even a short period of
certificate suspension.

Mechanic
ADMINISTRATOR V. CUSIC, ORDER EA-1898, APRIL
1983

Following overhaul of an engine on a Cessna 150,
the mechanic was charged with having made a
fraudulent entry in the maintenance records
relating to installation of new parts and
serviceable parts. The FAA issued an order
revoking the mechanic's certificate. The
mechanic requested a hearing before a law judge.
He tesitified on his own behalf, having no other

witnesses and was not represented by a lawyer. After reviewing the FAA's evidence, the judge affirmed the order of revocation. The mechanic then appealed to the full five-member National Transportation Safety Board, providing letters from three persons who purportedly had information favorable to the mechanic. The Board refused to consider this new evidence and affirmed the order of revocation.
EDITORIAL COMMENT: This mechanic clearly did not understand the procedures inherent in his appeal rights. He should have had the witnesses present at the hearing before the law judge to testify on his behalf. In failing to do so he, in effect, waived that right, since the full Board will not later review new evidence that could have been presented to the law judge.

Mechanic
ADMINISTRATOR V. HAWES, DOCKET SE-5668, APRIL 1983

The mechanic was charged by the FAA with having performed an annual inspection on a Cessna 150H in a manner not conforming to Section 43.15(a) of the FARs. A cylinder stud had pulled out due to a loose helicoil repair. The mechanic had failed to properly torque and test the stud for tightness during the earlier inspection. The FAA proposed to suspend the mechanic's license as well as his inspection authorization for a period of 60 days. After hearing all mitigating evidence, the law judge reduced the period of suspension to 35 days.

Business Operator
ADMINISTRATOR V. GUY AMERICA AIRWAYS, INC., DOCKET SE-5774, APRIL 1983

The FAA issued an emergency order revoking the respondent's air carrier operating certificate, alleging lack of proper requisite qualifi-

cations for such a certificate. At a hearing
before the law judge, the FAA called 23 witnesses
and the respondent called 17 witnesses. After
hearing all evidence, the judge found 12
violations of 26 FARs. They included operation
of a flight from JFK Airport to St. Maarten in
violation of the carrier's operating
specifications; allowing persons to ride in the
cockpit on 13 flights when the FAA had not
authorized such access; installation of an
engine starter without its air worthiness being
properly certified; operating a flight from JFK
to Montego Bay when there were no passenger
briefing cards in at least 5 seats; operating a
707 from Georgetown, Guyana to JFK Airport with
two children over the age of 2 years who were not
provided separate seatbelts; operating
approximately 354 flights in Boeing 707 aircraft
over a period of three months when it did not have
current enroute and approach and landing
information; operating a Boeing 707 on 3 flights
over water when it did not have two operable HF
transmitters aboard; operating 7 flights in a
707 to Havana, Cuba in violation of the operating
specifications; operating a 707 aircraft from
Havana, Cuba to San Juan, Puerto Rico with only
two trained and qualified flight attendants,
using an unqualified person as a third flight
attendant; operating approximately 398 flights
during a 3-month period when it did not have a
power plant condition monitoring maintenance
program as required by its operations
specifications; failure to provide a captain and
a first officer an adequate rest period upon
return to their home base from a series of
flights, and scheduling a flight engineer as a
crew member for a total of more than 12 hours
during a 24 hour period; used a pilot as pilot-
in-command of 3 flights between New York and
Georgetown, Guyana when the pilot had not been
observed by the FAA in the performance of his
duty as the pilot-in-command.

The law judge affirmed the FAA's order revoking
the carrier's operating certificate.

Pilot
HELMS v. DOWNING, EA 1861, January 1983.

A pilot was charged with flying a North American T28A on a photography mission over Atlanta in violation of FAR Section 91.39(d)(1). The purpose of the photography mission was to photograph a Convair 240 owned by Georgia Tech. The pilot flew at an altitude of 3000 feet and 500 feet above the Convair 240. The Georgia Tech campus formed part of the photograph backdrop.

The Convair pilot in preparation for the photography mission had earlier contacted an FAA inspector advising him of the intended flight and making inquiry as to appropriate altitudes for the mission. The violation charge was then filed based on operating a restricted category aircraft over a densely populated area without a certificate of waiver or special operating limitation.

The T38A airworthiness certificate contained a limitation stating "All flights, except for takeoff and landing, shall be conducted to avoid areas having heavy air traffic and to avoid cities, towns, villages and any other area where the flight will create hazardous exposure to persons and property on the surface."

The pilot's commercial certificate was suspended for a period of 90 days.

EDITORIAL COMMENT: Reliance should not be made on oral communications with employees of the FAA. Any required special permit or authorization should be secured in writing.

Pilot
HELMS v. CHIODO, Docket SE-5644, January 1983

The ATP pilot acting as pilot-in-command on an air taxi flight was charged with taking off from

the Arcadia, California airport, and operating
the aircraft beneath the ceiling in a control
zone without an IFR clearance. Cloud ceiling
was reported as 800 feet overcast at the time.

The pilot had requested an IFR clearance to on
top of the clouds. A substantial delay was
encountered, after which he departed without
receiving a clearance, contending that he was
able to remain in VFR conditions.

The FAA proposed to suspend the pilot's ATP
certificate for a period of 90 days. The law
judge took into consideration that the pilot's
certificate was his only means of livelihood and
reduced the suspension period to 20 days.

Pilot
HELMS c. NEELY, Docket SE-5636, January 1983

The FAA issued an order suspending the private
pilot's certificate for a period of 60 days.
The pilot was charged with operating an aircraft
within the airport traffic area of Montgomery
Field, California, without establishing and
maintaining two-way radio communication with
the ATC tower. He was charged also with not
holding and having in his possession a current
valid airman's medical certificate.

During a hearing before a law judge, the pilot--
who was not represented by an attorney--admitted
he did not have a medical certificate, and that
his aircraft was within 1-1/2 miles of the
control tower before he established two-way
radio communication with that facility.

The judge found no extenuating or mitigating
circumstances and, thus, sustained the FAA's
order of suspension for a period of 60 days.

Pilot
HELMS v. FINCHER, Docket SE-5571, January 1983

A private pilot holding multi-engine and instrument ratings was charged with three separate violations: (1) violation of an ATC clearance after departure from Hobby Airport, Houston, Texas; (2) striking the wing of a Cessna 310 while taxiing to a parking spot at Ruston Airport, Louisiana; (3) failure, when requested by an FAA inspector, to exhibit his airman's certificate and medical certificate.

The pilot's ATC departure clearance from Hobby Airport called for a turn to heading 040 degrees. The pilot instead continued a right turn to heading 240 degrees. This created a traffic conflict requiring a Southwest Airlines aircraft to be diverted.

After landing at Ruston Airport, the pilot was purportedly following directions of a flagman when the wingtip of his Cessna 421 struck the wingtip of a Cessna 310. When requested by an FAA inspector to exhibit his pilot's certificate and medical certificate, he was unable to locate them in his luggage, but produced a logbook instead.

After reviewing all evidence, the law judge affirmed the violation charges regarding ATC clearance deviation and the aircraft collision. The FAA did not prove its charges relating to the pilot's certificate and medical certificate. The judge took into consideration that the pilot was in Ruston for purposes of attending a funeral and that his emotional state might have interfered with his ability to immediately locate his certificates when requested to do so by the FAA inspector. The law judge then reduced the proposed license suspension from 90 days to a period of 75 days.

ILLUSTRATIVE AVIATION INSURANCE COURT CASES

AIRCRAFT HULL INSURANCE -- Colorado Court of Appeals, No. 82CA0079, O'Connor v. Proprietors Insurance Co. (September 30, 1982)

Following an accident in which an aircraft was damaged the owner filed a claim with his insurance company. The insurance company refused to pay and the owner sued. Decision: For the insurance company. The insurance policy contained a provision excluding coverage while the aircraft was "operated in flight in violation of the terms of its F.A.A. Airworthiness Certificate or Operational Record..." The aircraft had not received an annual inspection within the 12 months preceding the accident.

EDITORIAL COMMENT: Although the aircraft had recently received a 100 hour inspection, which was identical to requirements of an annual inspection, this did not satisfy requirements of the insurance policy. This case is a classic in that it demonstrates the necessity of reading all exclusions and conditions of a given policy before a loss occurs.

MISREPRESENTATION IN APPLICATION -- U.S. Court of Appeals, Fifth Circuit, No. 81-3709, Overturf v. Aero Insurance Agency, Inc. (September 24, 1982)

Following an accident in which his Cessna 310 multi-engine aircraft was damaged an owner was denied coverage and sued the insurance company. **Decision:** For the insurance company. The aircraft owner, who was piloting the aircraft at the time of the accident, was only a student pilot. He had misrepresented his pilot status when applying for insurance. This was a material fact upon which the insurance company had based its decision and action in issuing the policy, thus it was not required to pay for damage to the aircraft.

FLIGHT INSTRUCTION - Ranger Ins. Co. v. Ram Flying Club and Scott Davis and Scott A. Royer, Colorado Court of Appeals, No. 81CA1057, (July 29, 1982)

Student Pilot Royer and Instructor Davis undertook a flight in an aicraft operated by Ram Flying Club. The student received instruction during the first portion of the flight, after which the instructor assumed control of the aircraft. The aircraft crashed, injuring the student pilot, after which he sued the insurance company insuring the flight instructor and the flying DECISION: Against the student pilot, for the insurance company. The policy under which the club and the flight instructor were insured contained an exclusion for the bodily injury of any person who is a "pilot or crew member." The policy defined the words "pilot" or "crew" as "any person or persons involved in the operation of the aircraft while in flight." The judge ruled that student pilot Royer was a person involved in the operation of the aircraft while in flight and, therefore, was a crew member even though he was not operating the aircraft at the time of the accident. Thus, he could not recover against the insurance company.

EDITORIAL COMMENT: This does not necessarily mean the instructor or the flying club would not be legally liable for the student pilot's injury, but, rather that the insurance policy did not cover their liability. Thus, their personal assets would be subject to any judgment against them.

AIRCRAFT SALES -   IFR/VFR FLIGHT - Northwestern Flyers, Inc. and Cessna Finance Corporation v. Olson Bros. Mfgr. Co., U. S. Court of Appeals for the 8th Circuit, Nos. 81-1557, 81-1570, 81-1614, (June 17, 1982)

Northwestern Flyers, an authorized Cessna dealer, entered into a sales agreement with Olson Bros. for a 1979 Cessna Turbo 210 airplane. The sale price was $97,616.49. To finance its purchase, Northwestern borrowed $84,037.69 from Cessna Finance Corporation, which became a lienholder by retaining a security interest in the airplane. Northwestern's insurance policy was then made to show Cessna Finance Corporation an additional insured as a lienholder. Following transfer of title from Northwestern to Olson Bros., the aircraft was destroyed in an accident. Cessna Finance Corporation then made an insurance claim for the amount of its security interest based on the original financing transaction. DECISION: For the insurance company. Cessna Finance Corporation's insurance coverage was terminated upon transfer of title of the aircraft from Northwestern to the new owner, Olson Bros., and the new policy covering the aircraft did not include Cessna Finance Corporation as an insured.
Olson Bros. then filed a claim with its own insurance company for loss of the aircraft. The insurance company denied coverage on the basis that, at the time of the accident, the pilot was operating under instrument flight rules, although he did not have an instrument rating, and was, thus, in violation of a policy exclusion. Weather conditions prior to takeoff at both the departure point and the destination were VFR. While in route, the pilot reported flying at an altitude of 23,000 feet. Under Federal Aviation Regulations, instrument flight rules govern flight into air space above 18,000 feet. The insurance company contended that the flight in question became an IFR flight and the insurance coverage ceased when the pilot flew above that altitude. DECISION: For the aircraft owner, Olson Bros. The court would not accept the insurance company's argument. For purposes of this case, the court ruled that

weather conditions at the time of takeoff were
the criteria for characterizing the flight as
VFR rather than IFR. There was no evidence that
the pilot encountered actual instrument
conditions while flying above 18,000 feet.

TWO INSURANCE POLICIES, WHICH PAYS? - Figueroa
and Camps, et al. v. U. S. of America, U. S.
District Court for the District of Puerta Rico,
Nos. 81-1842, 81-2019, (January 4, 1983)

Pilot Villamil had secured a non-owner's
liability policy from Avemco Insurance Company.
With permission of the aircraft owner, he was
flying a Mooney, with passengers aboard, when
the aircraft crashed. The aircraft owner was
insured under a policy issued by Caribbean Star
Assurance Company. As a permissive user, the
pilot was an additional insured under the
owner's policy. A controversy arose between
Avemco and Caribbean Star Assurance Company as
to their respective liability under the policy.
The Avemco policy contained language limiting
its liability if "other insurance" covered the
same risk. The Star policy provided for a pro
rata sharing of liability if there was other
insurance. DECISION: Caribbean Star Assurance Company was the primary insurer, with
Avemco being an excess insurer for any judgment
amount above the Caribbean Star policy limit.

Caribbean alleged as a second argument why it
should not be held liable that the pilot and his
passengers were co-employees of Puerto Rico
Dairy, Inc. The policy contained an exclusion
for liability of one employee to another. The
court disagreed, however, on the basis that, in
this instance, the pilot was a direct insured
under the policy, rather than being insured as an
employee under his employer's policy.
EDITORIAL COMMENT: This case shows an example
of opposing policy interpretations of the type
frequently requiring litigation.

I-4

RENTER-PILOT - Doyen v. Cessna Aircraft Company,
Louisiana Court of Appeal, 3rd Circuit, No. 82-
55, (July 2, 1982)

A pilot rented a Cessna 172 from an airport
operator whose business included rental of such
aircraft. While under the pilot's control, the
aircraft crashed causing fatal injuries to
passengers. Survivors of the deceased
passengers brought suit against the pilot and
the insurance company insuring the business
operator who provided the aircraft. DECISION:
For the insurance company. The policy
contained a provision excluding coverage "to any
person operating the aircraft under the terms of
any rental agreement or training program which
provides any remuneration to the named insured
for the use of said aircraft." Thus, the
operator would have been covered for its
liability, but the pilot's liability while using
the aircraft under a rental agreement was not
covered.
EDITORIAL COMMENT: This case is quite typical
of aircraft rental situations in which the
renter-pilot's liability is not covered by the
aircraft owner's insurance policy. Although a
few states require coverage for a renter pilot be
included in the business operator's policy, many
pilots who fly aircraft owned by others are being
exposed to personal liability without realizing
it.

AIR TAXI FLIGHT - Insurance Company of the State
of Pennsylvania vs. West Plains, Inc.,
Missouri Court of Appeals, Southern District,
Division 1, No. 12301, (July 30, 1982)

A Beech A35 crashed in Iowa while carrying
passengers on an air taxi flight. The pilot had
not within the last 12 calendar months
accomplished a competency check as required by
Federal Aviation Regulations, Sec. 135.293.
The applicable insurance policy contained an

exclusion which stated the policy did not apply if the aircraft was being piloted by a pilot not property certificated, qualified and rated under the current applicable FARs for the operation involved. Suit was brought on behalf of the injured passengers. The insurance company refused to pay for their injuries. The basis for the refusal was the argument that the pilot "had not received her required checkride and certification from the Federal Aviation Administration." DECISION: For the passengers and against the insurance company. The pilot had previously met the minimum requirements of 750 logged solo flying hours, or as pilot-in-command, 100 hours in retractable gear aircraft, including 5 hours in the Beech A35. Acknowledging violation of the specific FAR, the court interpreted this violation as not having the effect of revoking or suspending the pilot's license or eradicating experience credits previously earned. Thus, the violation did not invalidate the insurance coverage of the policy.

EDITORIAL COMMENT: This case demonstrates a commonly applied principle relating to ambiguous provisions in insurance policies. Since an exclusion in effect takes away from coverage, the courts apply liberal interpretation rules to attempt to find coverage, rather than to exclude it. To be enforceable, exclusionary clauses must set forth clearly the basis for not providing coverage under the basic policy.

INSURANCE BROKER – Flagstaff Mortuary, Inc., v. Gamble, Arizona Court of Appeals, Division 1, No. 1CA-CIV5596, (January 13, 1983)

The owner of a Cessna 210 permitted a pilot to use the aircraft for a flight anticipated to be one hour and twenty minutes from Flagstaff, Arizona, to Phoenix, Arizona, and return. The pilot agreed to pay the owner $100 for use of the aircraft. On the return flight, the aircraft crashed and was badly damaged. Upon filing a claim, the owner's insurance company denied coverage on the basis that there was no coverage for the ill-fated flight. The owner then brought suit against the independent insurance agent who secured the policy alleging he was negligent in not securing a policy containing the same coverage as an earlier policy it replaced. The court was then called on to interpret the earlier policy to determine if it would have covered the aircraft damage had it still been in effect. DECISION: For the independent insurance agent and against the aircraft owner. The previous insurance policy contained a provision excluding coverage for "an operation for which a charge is made." The pilot had agreed with the owner of the aircraft to pay $100 for use of the aircraft on the flight from Flagstaff to Phoenix and return. The owner argued that this was a nominal fee for gas and maintenance and was not a "charge" in the usual sense. The court disagreed, stating, "The payment of anything more than reimbursement of the direct expenses of a flight is a charge and this is true regardless of whether such excess reflects a profit to the airplane owner or merely reimbursement for indirect costs, such as maintenance, insurance or depreciation."

EDITORIAL COMMENT: An aircraft owner who desires to allow selected persons to use an aircraft, paying for not only direct operating costs but including a reserve for maintenance, insurance and storage, should determine precisely what dollar amount would be adequate and then secure in advance from the insurance company a letter or policy endorsement stating that such payment would not be considered a "charge" so as to void the policy.

WHO IS COVERED? - Tubbs v. Compass Insurance

Company, Florida District Court of Appeal, 5th District, Case No. 81-993, (September 29, 1982)

Both Mr. & Mrs. Tubbs were killed in the crash of an aircraft piloted by Mr. Tubbs. The minor Tubbs children brought suit against the insurance company for death of their mother. The insurance company denied coverage, alleging that the doctrine of interspousal and interfamily tort immunity barred any claims by the heirs of Mrs. Tubbs' estate. DECISION: The original trial judge agreed with the insurance company. The appeal court, however, disagreed on the basis that the childrens' claim was against the insurance company, rather than against the estate of their father. This issue was then appealed to the Florida Supreme Court for a decision which has not as of this date been issued. Thus, it still remains to be seen whether the minor children will be allowed to collect on the insurance claim for the death of their mother.

TWO OWNERS OF AIRCRAFT, ONE NOT COVERED - Ventre v. Pacific Indemnity Co., Louisiana Court of Appeal, 3rd District, No. 7966, (May 26, 1982)

The pilot-owner of a Fairchild aircraft agreed to the sale of a one-half interest in the aircraft to a second pilot who was to make payment in installments. The original owner obtained a binder for insurance, naming both pilots as authorized to fly the aircraft. After the purchasing pilot's first installment payment check was returned for insufficient funds, the original owner-pilot became dissatisfied and decided not to go through with the deal. He then called the insurance agent and had the second pilot's name removed from the binder. The second pilot, nevertheless, obtained possession, flew and crashed the aircraft shortly thereafter, resulting in total loss. The insurance company denied coverage for the loss and was then sued by the original owner. DECISION: For the insurance company, against the aircraft owner. The pilot flying the aircraft at the time of the accident was not insured under the policy, since his name had been previously removed. The original owner argued that the pilot flying the aircraft was a thief having no right to fly the aircraft, and under the policy damage resulting from theft was covered. The court disagreed, however, pointing out that, under Louisiana law, the second pilot became a part-owner at the time of the original agreement and remained so at the time of the accident, even though his first installment payment check had been dishonored and the original owner had a change of mind regarding completing the transaction. Thus, the second pilot was not a thief since he was owner of one-half of the aircraft, but he was not named in the policy as an insured. This meant the insurance company did not have to pay for loss of the aircraft.

WHO IS INSURED? - Rick, Smith, et al. v. National Union Fire Insurance Co. and compass Insurance Co., Arizona Court of Appeals, Division 1, Nos. 1CA-CIV5374 and 1CA-CIV6047, (November 9, 1982)

These two cases were consolidated for trial because they contained identical issues regarding renter pilots. In separate accidents a Cessna and a Gruman American Model AA5A crashed, causing death to their occupants. Both business operators who rented the aircraft to the pilots were insured by insurance policies containing use provisions for "rental to pilots". An exclusion, however, excluded "renter pilots" from being insured by the policy. Suit was brought against the insurance companies by representatives of the deceased. DECISION: For the insurance companies. Although representatives for the deceased pilots' estates argued that these provisions

were ambiguous and should not be enforced so as
to deny coverage, the court disagreed, finding
no inconsistency between a declaration that
rental to pilots is a permissible use and that
renter pilots were not insured.

EDITORIAL COMMENT: This case demonstrates the
frequently confusing question of who is insured
under a policy while flying as a pilot, as
opposed to who is permitted to fly under terms of
the policy with only the aircraft owner being
an insured.